SCALE

ook of

ING

The Airfix book of
SCALE MODELLING

Jonathan Mock

CONWAY

A Conway Book

Text © Jonathan Mock, 2010
Volume © Conway, 2011
First published in Great Britain in 2011 by
Conway, an imprint of
Anova Books Company Ltd
10 Southcombe Street
London W14 0RA

To receive regular email updates on
forthcoming Conway titles, email
conway@anovabooks.com with 'Conway
Update' in the subject field.

British Library Cataloguing in Publication
Data
A record of this title is available on request
from the British Library

ISBN 978--184486-126-2

745.59

Distributed in US and Canada by:
Sterling Publishing Co., Inc
387 Park Avenue South
New York, NY 10016–8810

The content of this book is the result of the
authors' own research and reflects their
individual opinions. Both author and
publisher would welcome the contributions
of readers with further information relating
to the subject and they can be contacted
accordingly at the address given above.

Printed and bound by Craft Print
International Ltd, Singapore

www.anovabooks.com
www.conwaypublishing.com
www.airfix.com
Published with kind permission of Airfix, a
registered trade mark of Hornby Hobbies
Ltd.

Also available from Conway: *James May's
Toy Stories: The Airfix Handbook* (**978 1 844
861163**), *James May's Toy Stories: The
Scalextric Handbook* (**978 1 844 861170**),
The Hornby Book of Model Railways (**978 1
844 860951**) and *The Hornby Book of
Scenic Railway Modelling* (**978 1 844
861125**)

Picture Credits

Contents

FOREWORD

As editor of the old *Airfix Magazine* from 1965-72, and again from 1978-82, all the chapters of this nicely produced new book bring back many memories, usefully combining history with practical modelling. Back in the 1969-72 period I also edited the first *Airfix Annual*, and some of the first specialist Airfix publications that are mentioned in this book. In 1968 I wrote *How To Go Plastic Modelling*, one of the first books dealing specifically with plastic kit building.

I'm sure older readers of the *Airfix Book of Scale Modelling* will also have nostalgic memories of their younger years as keen plastic kit modellers, and like me will be reminded of models and projects half-forgotten from those earlier decades.

One thing this book demonstrates is the vast size of the plastic kit market today, and the sophistication of most of the larger-scale kits. In earlier days such developments were beyond our imagination. In the early 1960s, as I well recall, it was possible to make each new Airfix aircraft, ship or tank kit as they appeared, at well-spaced intervals. Today the output of new releases from Airfix alone, quite apart from other ranges, makes this impossible. Today, too, many variants of classic types such as the Spitfire are produced. Thirty or more years ago far more conversion work (as covered in Chapter 7) was needed to make further variants from one basic kit. Indeed, each issue of *Airfix Magazine* featured conversion projects, and if you want proof that plastic models will last out your lifetime, I still have all the Airfix kit conversions I made between 1961 and 1982 (plus a few more since), over 150 in all, still looking good in two large showcases.

Readers of this excellent new book should find all the inspiration they need to carry on the plastic modelling tradition for a good few decades yet!

Chris Ellis, 2010

A. Tooby

INTRODUCTION

When I started secondary school back in 1978 I came across a copy of *How to Go Plastic Modelling* by Chris Ellis in the school library. To say this book had a profound effect on my fledgling modelling skills is an understatement. Aside from the odd copy of *Airfix Magazine*, *Scale Models*, or *Military Modelling* (when the local newsagent stocked them), reading about the hobby was a rarity for a keen 11 year-old. But there in one volume was everything I needed – wanted – to know, a tantalising glimpse of what could be achieved with patience and practice. Tools, techniques and products I'd never heard of, with plenty of practical, and more importantly accessible, projects to try out. I took the book out on the first day I started school and renewed it repeatedly until I left in 1985 – these days I have my own copy!

The modelling scene has changed immeasurably since Chris wrote his book over forty years ago, not only in terms of the quality, quantity and variety of kits, but with regard to the equipment, techniques and technology available to modellers. Where once there was a dearth of modelling magazines there is now a positive glut. Where Europe and America used to dominate the kit market, Japan, China and nations from the former Eastern Bloc have

now emerged. Where contact with other modellers was limited to a local club or a model show, people can now talk, share and exchange information and advice at the click of a button.

The standard of modelling has also reached levels of detail and realism unthinkable decades back as each new generation brings in their own new ideas and techniques. But even those highly talented modellers started from somewhere using the most basic of tools, techniques and kits, and it is those basics that have remained essentially the same through the decades.

There are many books out there are written by and for the more advanced modeller, and these are truly inspirational. This book is aimed more at those either coming in to the hobby anew, who perhaps have already made a few kits and are looking to improve their skills, or those who have returned to the hobby after a while away and just need a primer on how to get started again.

For anyone new to the hobby these days it may seem a daunting and expensive prospect, with a bewildering array of kits, tools, accessories and paints available in model shops or online, and no end of advice that, though well meant, can lead to information overload. But modelling need not be complicated or expensive; in fact,

when compared with some other hobbies, getting started in modelling need not cost a lot of money – a basic tool kit, paints and kit can be had for very little expense.

We'll explain the basic tools, techniques and how to overcome or avoid the kinds of problems that every modeller will face. We'll also look at the choice of kits out there, the different scales, how kits are made and include some practical examples that you can join in with using the same kits, or indeed use as the basis for your own model projects.

Chris Ellis wrote that modelling is relaxing, therapeutic, educative, inexpensive and interesting, but above all fun. Forty years on that holds true more than ever. It is your hobby – enjoy it.

AUTHOR ACKNOWLEDGEMENTS

This book was very much a collaborative effort and my immediate thanks go to fellow contributors Brian Canell, Adam Cooper and Drewe Manton.

I am also grateful to everyone at Hornby Hobbies for their support and encouragement; Darrell Burge, Dale Luckhurst, Karen Redwood, Scott Elsey, Matt Whiting, Carl Hart and Trevor Snowden.

Personal thanks go to Hector and Judy Hamer, Tim A Maunder, Tim Perry, John Bank, Andrew Farmer, John Walker, Dave Fleming, Bill Clark, Spencer Pollard, Karin Breiter, Antics, The Airfix Tribute Forum, Frome Model Centre, Laurie Goodall and finally Lisa and Laura at the Corner Café who kept the tea coming.

And, of course, special thanks go to my family, least not my father for starting me off in the first place and my mother for encouraging me in all my artistic endeavours.

Dedicated to Mr Stinks.

Jonathan Mock 2010

CHAPTER 1

To begin at the beginning

HOW IT ALL BEGAN

For most people Airfix invented the plastic model kit. This may be slightly disingenuous, although Airfix certainly popularized plastic modelling in the public consciousness to the point that the name has come to mean any plastic kit, regardless of manufacturer, just as Thermos, Hoover and Xerox are now synonymous with any vacuum flask, vacuum cleaner or photocopier, respectively. Tell people that you're into scale modelling and they may get what you mean, tell them you make Airfix kits and they will know exactly what you mean.

People started making replicas of tanks and aeroplanes from wood well before they became available as commercial models. One of the pioneers of the model kit was Skybirds in England who settled on a scale of 1:72 (we'll look at scales a little later) for their range of aircraft. Their kits comprised of roughly shaped wooden parts – a genre that became known as 'solids' owing to the fact they were made from solid wood – and required sanding and shaping to get the basic outline, and then sealing to fill the wood grain before painting could start. Suffice to say that making even a basic single-engined aircraft would involve many hours or work before the model started to look the right shape. But Skybirds proved

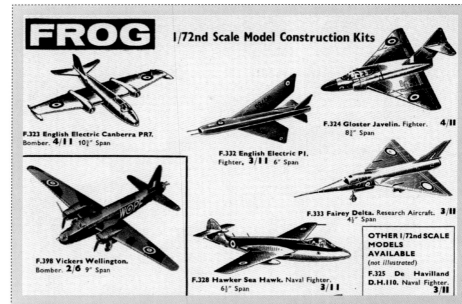

Fig 1.1 A press advert from the late 1950s for FROG, who pioneered plastic model aircraft with their 1:72 'Penguin' range in the mid-1930s.

popular, and to some extent this could be ascribed to their decision to stick to 1:72, enabling modellers to build up a collection of aircraft that were all to a constant scale. The range expanded to include airfield accessories alongside a mix of biplanes and (the then emerging) monoplanes, both civilian and military.

But the invention of the plastic kit really belongs to another English manufacturer,

FROG, who began life by making flying models in the early 1930s, hence the acronym Flies Right Off (the) Ground: F–R–O–G. In 1936 FROG started making a new line of plastic construction kits, a range marketed as 'Penguin' kits so as to distinguish them from the range of flying models. Why Penguin? Well penguins don't fly!

FROG also adopted the scale of 1:72 as pioneered by Skybirds, and the Penguin kits were very basic – the plastic used was a cellulose acetate butyrate, totally different to today's high impact polystyrenes, but in their time a revelation when compared to the 'solids'. Frog's pre-moulded parts meant a Spitfire could be built, painted and flying sorties around the living room in a single evening! Like Skybirds, FROG also developed a range of accessories to complement their aircraft, even including a massive hangar kit.

By a peculiar twist of fate, the Second World War heralded great advancements in the manufacture of plastics and injection moulding technology, with Germany leading the way. FROG continued to make models for the War Office and these were used as recognition aids. Post-war the Penguin kits did return but by the mid-1950s they were discontinued in favour of a new range of kits made from polystyrene – but they were no longer the only game in town.

ENTER AIRFIX

Founded in 1939 by Nicholas Kove, a Hungarian émigré, Airfix was the first company to bring injection moulding technology to Britain. Ironically, Airfix's name was never derived from anything to do with aircraft or models, but rather a personal penchant of Kove who, according to Airfix historian Arthur Ward, liked words ending in 'fix' and wanted his company to begin with an 'A' so it would appear at the front of trade directories. Airfix's first

products were a diverse range of household items, mostly born out of Kove's eye for a sales opportunity that made use of scant resources. At one point Airfix were the biggest manufacturers of plastic combs in the UK.

Airfix's entry into the world of plastic models came about in 1949 following a commission for a promotional model of a tractor by its makers, Ferguson. Ever the pragmatist, Kove suggested selling the unassembled parts to the general public. Ferguson saw this as a publicity coup and the first Airfix kit was born. Encouraged by what Kove saw as a new business opportunity, Airfix released a model of the *Golden Hind* in 1952, which arguably could be considered the first fully commercial Airfix kit. When Kove struck a deal with Woolworth's, one of the UK's biggest retail chain stores at the time, to sell bagged copies of their kits for a few pence each, suddenly kits became readily available and cheap – the modern era of plastic modelling was truly born.

The *Golden Hind* was a huge success and Kove was initially resistant to appeals from his General Manager, John Grey, to diversify into aircraft. Eventually they did and their first aircraft kit, a Spitfire Mk.I subsequently known as 'BTK', due to the spurious squadron code letters included (and seemingly modelled after Aurora's 1:48 kit) was released in 1953 (or 1955 – opinions vary!).

Fig 1.2 Classic Roy Cross box art for the Airfix *Golden Hind*, widely regarded as their first commercial plastic kit.

Of course the old hands felt this plastic revolution wasn't 'real modelling'; there was no skill needed with these moulded things and that it was a fad that would never catch on – but catch on it did and by the end of the 1950s plastic kits were appearing in force around the world and the days of the 'solids' were numbered.

Like Skybirds and FROG before them, Airfix settled on 1:72 as the preferred scale for model aircraft, 1:76 (or OO) for military vehicles and figures, 1:600 for ships, 1:32 for cars and larger model soldiers and 1:144 for airliners. They strongly promoted the 'constant scale' aspect of their products at a time when many of their rivals were scaling their kits to fit the size of the packaging.

Fig 1.3 Released in 1970, the Airfix 1:24 Spitfire 'Superkit' was one of the most ambitious kits of its era, especially when it came to moulding large, complex shapes. This artwork is from the 1990s boxing.

Fig 1.4 Published in 1960, *Airfix Magazine* was perhaps the first true journal aimed more at the plastic modeller.

With constant scale you could build up a collection of aircraft, ships and tanks with all the fascination in comparing sizes and shapes that it entails – by placing a Tiger Moth next to a Lancaster, HMS *Ajax* next to the *Admiral Graf Spee* or a Bren Carrier next to a Tiger Tank. For youngsters the availability, cheap retail price and easy construction made for great playthings, enabling the Battle of Britain or D-Day to be restaged in-between the football results and teatime on a Saturday afternoon.

To complement the kits Airfix also created its own range of oil based paints, initially sold in bottles before switching to tins (or tinlets) similar to those used by Humbrol. The colours were split between matt and gloss and older kits have references to paint codes such as M3, M6 or G8; fairly meaningless these days, but in their day most model and toy shops in the UK carried the range of Airfix paints and so the colours were (relatively) easy to figure out!

At its peak, the scope and range of the Airfix catalogue encompassed a variety of subjects for almost all modelling tastes: military 1:72 aircraft dominated, followed by ships, armoured fighting vehicles, cars, motorbikes, buildings, soldiers, trains, rockets, science fiction subjects, birds, historical figures and diorama play sets. Popular and well-known subjects like the Spitfire and Lancaster were represented in the range, but also lesser-known and unusual types like the experimental SR.53 rocket fighter and the SRN-1 hovercraft. If a Hawk jet trainer wasn't your cup of tea, a 1:1 Robin (*Erithacus Rubecula*) may well have

Fig 1.5 During the 1960s the magazine flourished and featured the groundbreaking conversion work of the late Alan W. Hall.

Fig 1.6 *Airfix Magazine* continued into the 1980s, but several changes of publishers led to its eventual demise in 1993.

Fig 1.7 In the 1970s a spin-off series of books were produced by Patrick Stevens Ltd, the (then) publishers of *Airfix Magazine*.

been. Similarly, you could make either a 1:12 Queen Elizabeth I (the monarch) or a 1:600 RMS *Queen Elizabeth 2* (the ship). Modellers could pick between an F-15 Eagle fighter or an Eagle Transporter (from the TV series *Space: 1999*).

Airfix consolidated their popularity in the 1960s when they released one of the first magazines aimed at plastic modellers called – naturally enough – *Airfix Magazine*. Running (on and off) right up until the early 1990s, the magazine introduced such famous names as Alan W. Hall, Chris Ellis and Bruce Quarrie as editors, and contributors like J.D.R. Rawlings, Alan Butler and Gerald Scarborough. As plastic modelling really took off there was a rich period of new kits running from the 1960s through to the mid-1970s and Airfix were releasing new models on a near-monthly basis, with the larger kits usually arriving just in time for Christmas. Airfix also consolidated its publishing ventures with an Airfix annual, and its own series of modelling guides that covered diverse subjects from armoured cars and Luftwaffe camouflage to Napoleonic wargaming and armies of the English Civil War. Larger books catered for more complex kits like the 1:24 Spitfire or HMS *Victory*. Airfix also formed its own 'Modellers' Club', and comic books of the 1970s memorably featured advertisements endorsed by the then club president Dick Emery, who was one of the most popular TV comic actors of that era.

For further reading on the history of Airfix, various books can be highly recommended; *The Boys' Book of Airfix* by Arthur Ward, Conway's *The Airfix Handbook* and *Airfix Kits* by Trevor Peak – see bibliography.

THE BOOM YEARS

Plastic modelling arrived at just the right time, both technologically and socially. Improvements in plastics meant that products could be moulded with more stability and durability, while manufacturers looking for inspiration had not only the Second World War to draw from, the heroics of which were still fresh in the minds of those who lived through it, but also advances in aircraft design (both military and civil), automobiles, ships and the new frontier – space.

While post-war Britain and much of Europe was still emerging from the shadows of rationing and reconstruction, in America there was a new optimism and affluence, especially amongst the younger generation, and plastic modelling equally gained new ground. Companies like Aurora, AMT, Hawk, Jo-Han, Lindberg, MPC, Monogram, Pyro, Lifelike and Revell became household names in the USA.

The range of kits on offer to the American modeller was more diverse, and perhaps less conservative, than their British counterparts. A classic example of this is Aurora, whose range of kits, though primarily dominated by more traditional subjects (cars, aircraft, and ships) are perhaps best remembered for their

Fig 1.8 This 1:72 Dornier Do 17 was one of a number of Italaerei (now Italeri) kits that were reboxed by Revell in the 1970s.

historical knights and movie/television tie-ins, featuring hardware from TV shows like Lost in Space, Voyage to the Bottom of the Sea and Batman. Aurora also produced kits of famous comic book figures like Superman, Superboy and Dick Tracy and of movie monsters like Dracula, Frankenstein, The Wolfman, King Kong and Godzilla. They even created a memorable range of dinosaur kits including their 'Prehistoric Scenes' series that came with diorama bases that could interlink to create one large scene – considerable palaeontological license was involved in mixing the various prehistoric eras with cavemen, although it is doubtful that many younger modellers either noticed nor cared!

Unsurprisingly, a lot of US kit manufacturers' ranges were dominated by car models – the automobile industry in

Fig 1.9 Monogram's 1:72 P-51B Mustang showing different packaging styles from the 1970s (top) and 1980s (bottom).

America was experiencing a boom period and many companies were only too happy to assist model manufacturers with what they saw as an excellent opportunity for free publicity. The model car market catered for everything from coupés, saloons and station wagons past and present to racing cars, hot rods and dragsters, haulage trucks, fire engines and pick-up trucks.

While AMT, Revell and Monogram all had healthy selections of automobiles in their catalogues, Revell were amongst the first US companies to develop a large range of 1:72 aircraft that featured stalwarts like the Spitfire and Messerschmitt Bf109,

Fig 1.10 Dramatic box art from Hasegawa's 1:72 Jaguar GR.1 kit first released in the 1980s.

complemented by the more unusual Fiat CR.42 Falco biplane and the PZL P.11C parasol-winged fighter. Monogram's 1:48 aircraft became known for their detail and completeness, and sometimes their size, though it was their 1:72 B-36 Peacemaker that was at one stage known as 'the largest plastic kit in the world'. AMT were the first kit company to release *Star Trek* related models starting with a kit of the USS *Enterprise* (AMT kits of the starship *Enterprise* subsequently featured in the TV series), an association that continued right through to the *Star Trek* movies and *The Next Generation* and *Deep Space Nine* TV shows.

Europe was also developing its own kit culture, Italy being able to boast three brands with ESCI, Italaerei (now Italeri) and Supermodel. ESCI's line encompassed some

notable kits, namely their 1:9 Kubelwagen and BMW R-75 motorbike, but it was their huge 1:72 military range for which they became best known. Italeri were amongst the pioneers of 1:35 scale armour and figures, but they also developed some fine 1:72 aircraft kits including WWII gliders like the Horsa, WACO Hadrian, Gotha 242 and the mammoth Messerschmitt Me 323 Gigant. Supermodel is best remembered for their 1:72 range of Italian fighter, bomber and floatplane aircraft, not to mention the sleek Blohm and Voss BV138 flying boat.

But it was in Japan that plastic kits really took off, not only in terms of popularity but also in terms of technological innovation, with Tamiya and Hasegawa leading the way, along with Nitto, Fujimi, ARII, Otaki, Bandai and Marusan. These days

the likes of Hasegawa and Tamiya are considered benchmarks of excellence, a position attained through generations of family ownership that has ensured a continuity of culture and investment, but in the early days of plastic modelling kits from Japan tended to be dismissed as 'toy-like' or 'not up to western standards' – the Japanese manufacturers learned fast!

Like their western counterparts, the Japanese kit companies also developed varied ranges, mainly built around aircraft, cars, ships and military subjects. And while Tamiya and Hasegawa have aspects of their ranges that overlap, notably with their 1:24 cars, 1:48 aircraft and 1:350 and 1:700 ships, Hasegawa have rarely ventured into 1:35 military subjects while Tamiya's 1:72 aircraft line is modest and mostly limited to WWII subjects. In fact, Tamiya's range is mostly known for their 1:35 military vehicles and figures – their German 88mm gun is reputed to be one of their best selling kits of all time – but they are also dominant in the radio-controlled car market and have a sideline in educational and scientific models. Always looking to improve and innovate, one of Tamiya's most impressive moulding feats in recent years has been their 1:48 Fieseler Storch, which featured the fuselage and side-canopies moulded as a single tan-coloured and clear plastic piece.

Hasegawa on the other hand have tended to concentrate more on 1:72 and

Fig 1.11 Beast from the East – science fiction subjects are very popular in Japan, this kit by Bandai depicts 'King Gidrah' from the Godzilla movies.

1:48 aircraft, along with 1:72 military subjects (an area Tamiya have rarely ventured into, if ever). Perhaps one of Hasegawa's more famous, certainly most impressive, ranges is their 'Museum Series' of kits like the 1:16 Wright Brothers Flyer or 1:8 Sopwith Camel, Fokker Triplane and Royal Aircraft Factory SE5A, massive replicas that are constructed from separate ribs and spars just like the originals and designed to be left uncovered to show off all the detail.

Bandai are not only arguably the biggest kit and toy company in the world, but they are also an entertainment giant, with subsidiaries involved in video games and anime (animated TV shows and films). And while in the past they have produced 1:24 aircraft and 1:48 armour and figure kits, Bandai are perhaps best known for their *Gundam* range of science-fiction robot kits, toys and other licensed products. The total *Gundam* phenomenon is huge in Japan and as of 2008 was worth 50 billion yen (£370 million or US $500 million at 2010 rates). A notable innovation in the *Gundam* range is the ability to mould parts in different colours on the same sprue, meaning younger modellers can put together a kit with the minimum of fuss.

Coloured plastic was also a feature of the Matchbox company – famous for their die-cast car models – who launched a range of plastic kits in 1973 that came with the sprues moulded in different colours with 'no painting required', if you didn't mind a Spitfire with a brown fuselage and green wings! Matchbox also offered alternative decal schemes as standard and even optional parts, their 1:72 Hawker Tempest scoring over the rival Revell and FROG kits by including the radial engined variant and Indian Air Force markings. Like Airfix they also created a range of polythene soldiers in both 1:76 and 1:32, while their 1:76 AFV range went one better by including a miniature diorama base with each model. Though Matchbox made sure they had the usual 'bankable' subjects like Spitfires, Hurricanes, Me Bf109s, FW190s, P-51D Mustangs and Mitsubishi Zeros for the mass market, they also found time to make the more unusual – and hitherto never produced – subjects for the enthusiast like the Hawker Fury (their first kit), AW Siskin, Fairey Seafox and Percival Provost.

CONSOLIDATION AND REBIRTH

Sadly, the oil crisis of the 1970s and world-wide recession of the 1980s saw raw materials and production costs rise, and coupled with shrinking markets many of those plastic pioneers faded from view. Aurora were among the biggest casualties in the USA while in the UK it was FROG who fell by the wayside, the tooling having been sent to Russia and the kits reborn as NOVO before they too ceased trading. Airfix also nearly disappeared. Even though the kit side of the business was still making money (albeit down on the boom years), problems within Airfix Industries and other brands and products that it owned had caused so many major losses and shortfalls in cash flow that, in 1981, Airfix called in the receivers – luckily there were no end of buyers looking to take on the famous name and Airfix was sold on, first to Palitoy and then eventually to Humbrol Ltd.

The 1980s is generally seen as perhaps the quietest decade for the hobby as all the major kit manufacturers pared back their ranges and new kit releases slowed down against the rise of competition from computer games, Walkmans and video recorders. Despite a period of economic austerity there were still some quite notable kits being produced; like the Avro Vulcan from Airfix and Handley Page Heyford and Victor from Matchbox, while Monogram released a full-stack version of their giant 1:72 Space Shuttle with fuel tank and solid rocket boosters. Revell went one better and brought out a massive 1:48 kit of the equally massive Rockwell B-1B bomber!

While the major companies rode out the economic storm, it was in the 'cottage company' or aftermarket accessory field where the real revolution was taking place, with small – often home-based – companies offering modellers detail or conversion parts in resin, white metal and photo-etched brass. Pioneers like PP Aeroparts and Aeroclub led the way for the incredible variety of products that now exist, offering almost any and every kind of accessory part for aircraft, ships, cars and military subjects.

Some companies, like Merlin and Pegasus in the UK, went further and offered their own complete plastic kits – they were admittedly sometimes rather basic and aimed at the more experienced modeller, but as the technology improved and more companies started producing their own kits, the quality soon began to catch up with the mainstream manufacturers.

By the end of the 1980s the hobby seemed to catch a second wind, an impression reinforced by the emergence of some new companies, most notably Dragon from Hong Kong, Hobbycraft from Canada, Academy from South Korea and Trimaster and Fine Molds from Japan. The thawing of the Cold War in the 1990s saw many exciting new kit companies emerging from the former Czechoslovakia and USSR whilst the 21st century has seen China emerge as a force to be reckoned with in the modelling world. New names continue to join the ranks of Airfix, Revell, Hasegawa and Tamiya and include Eduard, ICM, Trumpeter, Tasca, Bronco, Great Wall and Hobbyboss, with still more companies emerging and offering high quality models.

In 2006 Airfix looked again to be facing oblivion in circumstances that almost mirrored those of 1980/81 – Airfix was profitable, but its parent company Humbrol suffered cash flow and supply problems and so Airfix was up for sale again. This time Hornby stepped in to add this famous brand to its own heritage and that of Scalextric, the well-known slot-car racing brand. In an ironic twist, the Airfix headquarters at Hornby's facilities in Margate is also the site of the former FROG factory.

WHAT'S IN A BOX?

While many of those great names have passed into history, their products live on either as tooling that has been acquired by another company, or as a run of mouldings that are simply repackaged. In some markets there may be distribution or licensing deals that result in kits being reboxed; for example in Japan some Monogram kits have been sold as Hasegawa products in the past, and Italeri have a deal with Tamiya who rebox the Italian manufacturers' kits as their own. Even for experienced modellers it can sometimes be hard to keep track of which kit is in what box.

FROG were one of the first kit companies to expand their own range by either leasing tooling, or getting kits moulded for them, by other companies. The early FROG range included kits from Heller in France and Renwal in the USA. More famously FROG struck a deal with Hasegawa and the two companies traded kits for several years, along with some car kits by AMT. FROG kits then reappeared under the guise of NOVO in the late 1970s – essentially still FROG but relocated to Russia – but the Soviet authorities at the time took a dim view of what they saw as kits of 'fascist powers' (Germany, Italy and Japan) so most of this tooling ended up with Revell. Ironically, some FROG kits of Russian subjects (the MiG 3, Lagg 3, Yak 3 and Anatra DS) intended for the Russian market were never sent and ended up being issued by Red Star, a British company!

Revell have proved to be very adept over the years at reissuing other kits, having reboxed products from FROG, Heller, Lindberg, ESCI, Monogram, Italeri, Matchbox, Fujimi and Hasegawa to name but a few. Matchbox themselves incorporated chunks of the AMT range in the late 1970 when the two were part of the same group. Moreover, some old Otaki aircraft kits in the late 1980s were in turn also reissued by AMT.

Airfix reboxed some 1:35 Max military vehicle kits from Japan in the 1970s, which was picked up by Italeri who also rebox many ESCI kits as well as models by the American company Accurate Miniatures and MPM from the Czech Republic.

Airfix's famous range of railway kits had their origins with another British manufacturer, Rosebud Kitmaster. Subsequently a lot of those railway tools ended up with Dapol. Airfix also reissued some MPC kits, mainly cars and *Star Wars* models in the 1980s – the Hawk and Eagle spacecraft from *Space:1999* were originally MPC kits. In more recent years Airfix have incorporated kits by Heller, Italeri, Academy, Otaki, Trumpeter and MPM. Academy have reissued some models by Hobbycraft from Canada; Eduard and Bilek in the Czech Republic have also released some Airfix kits.

As you can see, it can sometimes be very confusing to keep tabs of just what kit you might get in a box, but help is at hand!

CLUBS AND ORGANISATIONS

There are several long running clubs and organisations that exist to help modellers, foremost of which is the International Plastic Modellers' Society, formed in England in 1963, which now has branches worldwide, most of whom have regular meetings, organize shows and have their own national and local magazines and newsletters, websites and forums. The IPMS also has 'Special Interest Groups' or 'SIGs' that focus on specific subjects like the Harrier, F1 and Motorsport, Sci-Fi and Fantasy, Aircraft Carriers and Armour – there is even a SIG dedicated specifically to Airfix Modelling.

In the UK the IPMS Nationals show or 'IPMS Nats'– now known as Scale Model World – is recognised as one of the world's largest model shows, taking place over a weekend in the autumn of every year, and is complimented by many local IPMS branch shows, large and small, and several key (non-IPMS) model shows up and down the country, such as Southern Expo and Euro Militrae. This is also echoed around the world with the IPMS (USA) nationals and chapter shows, model shows in France, Belgium, Germany, the Czech Republic, Hungary, Russia and more as well as huge extravaganzas in Japan, including the annual trade fair at Shizouka where kit companies from around the world come to announce and display new or forthcoming releases.

Other model organizations of note in the UK include the Miniature Armoured Fighting Vehicle Association (MAFVA) and the British Model Soldier Society (BMSS), while in the USA there is the Armor Modeling and Preservation Society (AMPS).

The modern version of the old Airfix Modellers' Club is Club Airfix, where members receive a quarterly magazine, special offers and the chance to purchase exclusive (and collectible) kits made for club members only. Airfix also run the very popular make-and-take events at air displays and model shows where budding modellers get the chance to make and paint a model for free.

WHAT MAKES A MODELLER?

Humans like to do things with their hands – be it painting, crafts, gardening, playing music, writing, carving, woodworking or building. The instinct is strong and immediate. Even before basic languages and the written word had been developed, there was a desire to make things. The early cavemen developed skills to hunt, build and make fire in order to stay alive, but they also found time to make jewellery and art. The need to replicate objects in miniature also dates back thousands of years, from the face on a coin to a statue of a horse. Psychologists would say that our desire to create things in miniature is a controlling mechanism, a need to create order and make sense of our world – but it could also be because it is great fun.

As with any hobby where precision is required, modelling can help us learn and develop valuable skills that carry over into the rest of our daily lives, from hand-eye coordination to concentration, neatness, method and patience. With modelling we not only get the tactile satisfaction of creating something but also the artistic pleasure of painting it, whether this is a simple kit made straight from the box or a model heavily-

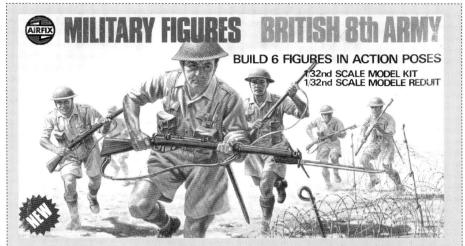

Fig 1.12 Released in 1975, Airfix's 1:32 Multipose range enabled modellers to build figures in a variety of poses with a choice of head gear, weapons and equipment.

modified or super-detailed. Researching the history of a subject and how it works not only expands our knowledge and understanding, but also hones our learning capabilities.

People also make models for different reasons; for some it is a simple diversion from the day job, for others it is the challenge of trying to recreate something in the most meticulous detail. Some people are drawn to particular subjects and build up collections based on a theme or era, e.g. US aircraft of the Vietnam War, or even the development of one subject like the Tiger tank and its many production variants and colour schemes. Others just like the variety of making a car one week, a ship the next.

There is also the appeal of creating dioramas, models placed within a scenic setting that tell a story, whether it is an aircraft being refuelled between sorties or tanks entering a bombed-out street in Europe. You may spend a couple of evenings working on a project or several months.

Box art also plays a big part in shaping our choices on what we buy and build, which, after all, is the intention. The fabulous Airfix box-top paintings by Roy Cross are considered classics of their genre and inspired several generations to buy and make models based purely on the story being played out on the box lid, perhaps of subjects they may not have previously had an interest in – the sight of a lone

Fig 1.13 'G for George' only just making it back to base, perhaps one of the most iconic of box tops produced by Roy Cross.

Wellington bomber limping home on one engine, chased by Bf109s, or the Tirpitz engaged in battle with all guns blazing. These evocative scenes appeal to the imagination. Some modellers have even put their return to the hobby down to seeing the box art of their youth still going strong decades later – for example, such was the nostalgia and admiration of the famous painting of 'G for George', which shows an Avro Lancaster landing with one engine ablaze, that Airfix

resurrected the box art for a special reissue of their Lancaster kit. This same artwork is also one of the most consistently popular images for other Airfix merchandise like greetings cards and drinks coasters.

COLLECTING

Like other hobbies, modelling also has its highly collectable aspects, either in forming a group of finished models that show fighters of the RAF, German

ships of the Second World War, American 'muscle' cars or military vehicles of the Gulf War. A collection may be centred around just one subject, perhaps showing the development of the Spitfire from the original prototype K5054 to the Seafire 47, or perhaps the Seafang and Spiteful variants. Or maybe the history of the Messerschmitt Bf109, Focke Wulf 190, Sherman tank or Willys Jeep. Not only is there the satisfaction and fascination of the aesthetic differences in shapes, sizes and colours, but there is also the educational aspect of seeing how technology develops, from fabric-covered biplanes to metal-clad jet planes, or wooden galleons to nuclear-powered aircraft carriers.

Model soldier collections can be similarly vast and varied, with figures from different eras all representing a challenge in painting to bring them to life, or they may be focused on a single historical period or indeed campaign – like the Napoleonic Wars, the Battle of the Somme or the Russian Front.

But you don't have to make models to collect them, especially with kits that are either very rare or may never appear again, and many examples do end up preserved in their unmade form, historical snapshots not only of a company's products from a given period, but also encapsulating the styles of the time. Amongst the most highly sought-after Airfix kits are the Ferguson tractor, the original 'BTK' Spitfire, the MV *Free Enterprise* ferry and the SAM2 missile. Their scarcity and resultant value typically results from circumstance – usually because the original moulds are either lost or no longer capable of being used. Sometimes a mould may be irrevocably modified and it is no longer possible to manufacture the original version – when Airfix retooled its RAF C-130 Hercules moulds to make the

Fig 1.14 The first Airfix kit was originally produced as a promotional and sales tool for Ferguson tractors.

American AC-130 version, it meant that the original RAF kit could no longer be produced. Likewise the Airfix conversion of the BAC Canberra to the America B-57 version, or VC-10 airliner to the VC-10 K2 tanker. Some kits will never again see the light of day. One famous example are kits produced from a batch of Aurora moulds that had been purchased by Monogram Models in the USA. The moulds were damaged in a train derailment, rendered unuseable and thus were scrapped – subsequently the value of the 'lost' kits shot up on the collectors' market. The classic Airfix B-17 and Wellington kits

may well become collectible items for the future given that the tooling was retired due to the moulds being too worn for future production to be viable.

It is not just the kits that are collectable, however; amassing and cataloguing all the variations of box art and packaging is a hobby in itself. In this area, everything from the actual box art painting to the colour of the packaging or shape of the logo can be of great importance to the keen collector. Airfix's diverse packaging over the decades has evolved its own language, as people talk of a 'type 1 header' or a 'box type 2', with

Fig 1.16 Illustration by Adam Tooby of Mosquito FB Mk VI of No. 487 Squadron RNZAF, during the raid on Amiens prison in February 1944.

some kit boxes featuring almost imperceptible differences, even down to a minor change in typeface, but all very important to the keen collector. There are even groups like The Airfix Collectors Club, which publishes its own magazine called *Constant Scale*.

The very first mass-produced Airfix models started off in polythene bags –

the famous 'polybag' kits – stapled to a header card featuring a basic line drawing reproduced in block colours, with the instructions printed inside. As four colour litho printing technology became cheaper and more accessible, the artwork eventually evolved into full colour paintings on both the polybag kits and the boxed ones. In the 1970s Airfix

created the 'blister pack' for its Series 1 kits, an ingenious – and award winning – design, consisting of a single piece of card with the box art and colour scheme drawings printed on one side and assembly drawings on the reverse, the card being folded over with the kit parts sealed within a rigid moulded plastic cover.

By the end of the 1970s blister packs gave way to boxes. Box art was toned down — explosions and gunfire were removed due to changing social attitudes — before giving way to photographs of models in the 1980s. Many collectors and modellers consider this to be the low-point for Airfix, both historically and aesthetically — the drab packaging was a great comedown after the heights of the Roy Cross era, while the number of new releases had slowed to a crawl. When Humbrol acquired Airfix in 1986 it continued this type of photographic packaging before bringing back box art in 1988, initially with new artwork by, amongst others, James Golding and Terry Harrison, before reviving Roy Cross's famous artwork in the 1990s along with new compositions by the late Gavin McLeod.

The current signature red boxes of the Airfix range now feature the computer-generated artwork of Adam Tooby, who has bought new levels of realism and excitement — not to mention a highly collectable aspect — to Airfix's box art, and we'll be looking at how these are created in Chapter 3.

THE 21ST CENTURY

It is true that some kits today can seem prohibitively expensive but for the most part those that are tend to be highly detailed and often complex kits. Their retail prices reflect the incredible amount of research and development that has gone into the production. Recent kits like the 1:24 Airfix Mosquito top the £100 mark — although, with 617 parts, it is clearly not a weekend kit for a beginner!

It is equally true, however, that the market for affordable models has also never been better. Airfix, Revell, Italeri and Hobbyboss all offer easy to build and good value entry-level kits. Even some of the Japanese kits that may seem expensive in other parts of the world are moderately priced in their home market — and the Japanese market for plastic kits is huge, almost every major city having the kinds of well- stocked model shops that many western modellers can only dream of.

Certainly when compared to some other hobbies and pastimes, modelling typically offers excellent value for money, with even the cheapest, simplest kits capable of providing hours of entertainment spread over a period of days, or even weeks and months, while the cost of the more expensive kits can equally be offset by the time invested to make them.

While it could be argued that the demise of many traditional model shops could — perhaps should — have been detrimental to the hobby, the rise of the Internet has opened up the hobby enormously. It is perhaps no coincidence that as the internet has grown, and more and more modellers have found ways to communicate, and companies (both large and small) have discovered more effective and direct methods of marketing their goods — either via web sites or Facebook pages — the hobby has also grown in tandem to the point that now, in the second decade of the 21st century, it is enjoying what many consider to be a new 'golden era'.

CHOOSING A KIT

Fig 2.1 The kind of choice a well-stocked model shop can present to a modeller.

Fig 2.2 An example of a skill rating that helps as a guide to the complexity and suitability of a kit.

With the huge variety of kits available to the modeller, choosing the right one can be a daunting prospect, all the more so if you're lucky enough to have a well-stocked model shop to hand!

Many models bought for youngsters by well-meaning relatives who buy a kit on the strength of the price, box art or subject matter often do so with little regard to its suitability. It's often claimed that older, more basic kits might put a newcomer 'off modelling for life', perhaps because of the poor fit of parts, overdone surface detail, lack of absolute accuracy. Equally, however,

it could be argued that many a modern kit could do the same, particularly if it has a more complicated construction process or many delicate parts that might be fine in the hands of an experienced enthusiast, but frustratingly fragile for an inexperienced modeller. A biplane might look like an innocuous choice – virtually everyone has heard of the Red Baron's famous all-red Fokker DR.1 triplane – but trying to align wings and struts may be taxing for a newcomer. On the flipside a state-of-the-art tank kit with separate track links and photo-etched parts might be overly complex and require knowledge of tools and skills not yet mastered. So clearly choosing the *right* kind of model is important.

Some kit companies put a 'skill level' on

their boxes, Airfix and Revell most notably, along with a figure giving the number of parts, all of which gives a rough idea of the potential complexity and suitability of a kit. Both FROG and Matchbox used to grade their kits by colour, while Airfix mark their kits by series number, a handy way of gauging not only the price but also the relative complexity of kits, i.e. the lower the series number, the cheaper and easier the kits are likely to be – in theory!

A MATTER OF SCALE

Take a look at a kit box and you'll see a series of numbers presented as a ratio or fraction, for example 1:72 or ¹⁄₇₂. This is the scale of the model. The number '1' refers to real-life subject while the second set of figures – for example '72' – reflects the size reduction. So if the scale is listed as 1:72 that means the model is seventy-two times smaller than the real thing, or in other words it would take seventy-two 1:72 Spitfires laid wingtip to wingtip to equal the wingspan of the real Spitfire.

The larger the second set of numbers, the smaller the scale will be, so a 1:144 Spitfire will be much smaller than a 1:72 one (half the size, in fact), while a 1:48 Spitfire will be larger. Roughly speaking the larger the real life subject, e.g. a ship or aeroplane,

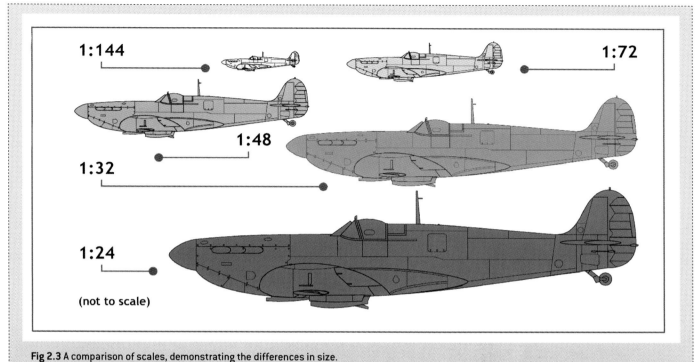

Fig 2.3 A comparison of scales, demonstrating the differences in size.

the smaller the scale tends be, though there are notable exceptions like the Airfix 1:72 Concorde or Revell's giant 1:72 U-Boat, both subjects usually found in the smaller scales.

Let's take a look at the most popular scales.

1:72

As mentioned earlier this scale was established by Skybirds in the 1930s and has remained the most popular scale for model aircraft. Derived from imperial measurements, where 1 inch equals 6ft, 1:72 and has proved versatile enough to allow smaller subjects (like a Spitfire) to be adequate in size with slightly larger subjects (say a Lancaster) being similarly manageable, though obviously there are plenty of large aircraft subjects that have not been produced in 1:72 simply because they would be *too* large (e.g. many airliners).

Hasegawa and ESCI also adopted 1:72 scale for tanks and AFV kits in the 1970s, at a time when most other kit companies (Airfix, Matchbox, Fujimi and Nitto) preferred 1:76 for their military vehicles. These days, 1:72 military subjects now outnumber their 1:76 counterparts with new kits coming from Dragon, Revell and Trumpeter amongst others. Many modellers are happy to mix 1:72 and 1:76 military subjects and the 4% difference between scales is only really noticeable if you were to place two models of the same subject together. It would take a very skilled modeller to really notice the

Fig 2.4 Airfix's range of 1:48 aircraft continues to expand and 2010 saw the release of this Messerschmitt Bf109E, finished as an E-1B bomber version.

scale difference between a 1:76 Kubelwagen placed next to a 1:72 Messerschmitt Bf109.

There have also been a number of maritime subjects in 1:72 from Airfix, Revell and Tamiya, with kits of Vosper MTBs, German E and S boats, PT boats, Air Sea Rescue Launches and RNLI lifeboats. Perhaps two of the largest examples are the 1:72 Flower Class Corvette originally made by Matchbox, and the 1:72 U-Boat and Gato class submarines made by Revell.

1:144

Exactly half the size of 1:72, 1:144 was chosen as a convenient way to reproduce larger subjects like airliners, allowing modellers to collect and compare the relative size differences between a De Havilland Comet and a Boeing 747. But 1:144 is not just the preserve of large aircraft; Revell released a range of 1:144 WWII fighter aircraft in the 1970s and have continued to develop the scale with subjects as diverse as airliners and military aircraft (large and small) to exotic subjects like

Russian Wing-in-Ground effect 'Ekranoplans'.

1:144 scale has also been used for space subjects, both fact and fiction, again primarily because kits can dovetail into aircraft collections and dramatically illustrate the size of a rocket next to a Boeing 737. Both Airfix and Revell have produced kits of the Saturn V (used in the Apollo moon landings) and the Space Shuttle in 1:144. Similarly, both Airfix and Aurora chose the same scale for their kits of the fictional Orion shuttle used in the movie *2001: A Space Odyssey*. It has even been adopted for a few maritime models like Revell's USS *Fletcher*, Lindberg's USS *Arizona* and Airfix's SRN-4 Hovercraft.

1:48

Known as 'quarter scale' because ¼ inch equals 1 foot, 1:48 mostly originated in the United States and was picked up by Aurora and Monogram for a lot of their aircraft kits. Over time Revell, Tamiya, Italeri, Hasegawa, ESCI and Airfix all adopted 1:48 and added aircraft kits to their ranges with newcomers Trumpeter and Hobbyboss also joining them.

In recent years 1:48 has also become a popular scale for armour models, perhaps as a crossover with aircraft modelling. Tamiya have built up a formidable range of subjects from the well known Tiger and Sherman tanks to the more unusual like the Komatsu tractor and Austin Tilly truck. For many modellers 1:48 scale armour provides a good compromise between high levels of detail (as is found in the larger 1:35 scale) and compactness.

1:32

Also known as '54mm' in model soldier circles, 1:32 was the most popular scale for figures, at least initially, thanks to Britains in England, Historex in France, a host of white-metal manufacturers and, of course, the famous Airfix range of polythene figures.

The Historex range, though scaled closer to 1:30, is famed for its highly detailed Napoleonic figures and accessories enabling modellers to interchange parts to create individual models. Airfix also released a range of historical model soldier figures from periods such as the Napoleonic era, English Civil War and the American War of Independence, along with mounted figures on horseback. Their 1:32 series of WWII 'Multipose' figures are still considered to be amongst the best model soldier figures ever made with their interchangeable parts and optional weapons and headgear. Both Airfix and Monogram tried to consolidate 1:32 as *the* scale for military modellers by introducing vehicle kits in the 1960s and 70s but, fine as those models were, 1:32 would eventually lose out to the wave of 1:35 kits coming from Tamiya, Italeri and ESCI.

Airfix and Matchbox also produced car kits to 1:32, some of these slotting in (in every sense) with Scalextric fans who adapted the models to take electric motors.

1:32 has proved more durable with aircraft modellers, with Revell establishing perhaps the largest choice of subjects, mainly WWII fighters and a few modern jets, a range that continues to be developed to this day with new kits like the Ju 88 and He 111. In recent years Tamiya have pushed the boundaries of kit manufacture with a superb 1:32 Mitsubishi Zero that was only eclipsed by their superlative 1:32 Spitfire MkIX. Trumpeter in China have also adopted 1:32 and have produced kits of hitherto never-released subjects like the Grumman Avenger and A-10 Thunderbolt.

1:35

The established scale for military models thanks to the pioneering efforts of Tamiya, Italeri and ESCI, not to mention the fabulous work of US modeller Shep Payne and Belgian modeller François Verlinden whose dioramas and finishing techniques inspired generations and revolutionised the hobby in so many ways. As mentioned earlier, Airfix briefly had a range of 1:35 kits in the late 1970s, mostly soft-skinned US vehicles that were repackaged kits originally made by Max from Japan.

1:35 received a boost in the late 1980s with the arrival of Dragon from Hong Kong who lead the way in the scale with frequent releases of complex and high quality kits – their reputation was perhaps cemented with

Fig 2.5 A Lee tank from Tamiya, who pioneered 1:35 as a scale. Despite its complex looks, this is one of their easier AFV models.

their 1:35 kit of the Scud missile and tractor, made famous by the Gulf War of 1991, that arrived in the model shops only months after the conflict had ended. Recent arrivals on the scene include Trumpeter along with other kit companies like Tasca, Bronco and Great Wall who are establishing reputations for high quality kits for the discerning enthusiast.

The range of 1:35 kits available nowadays is staggering and offers something for every taste and pocket, from a BMW motorbike to the incredible Dora railway gun, the largest (and perhaps most expensive!) plastic kit ever made. In between you can buy armoured cars, trucks, tanks, even railway locomotives and wagons, not to mention helicopters and of course a myriad of figures and diorama accessories. There are even maritime subjects available, notably Tamiya's modest 'Pibber' patrol boat from the Vietnam War and Italeri's mighty German S-Boat from WWII.

1:24

This scale is popular with car modellers (along with the almost identical 1:25), and Monogram, Revell, Tamiya, Italeri and Fujimi make kits of everything from Mini Coopers and VW Beetles to fire engines and juggernauts. 1:24 has also been adopted for aircraft models, with Airfix starting a range of 'Superkits' in 1970 with their ground-breaking Spitfire Mk.I through to their massive 1:24 Mosquito of 2009. Bandai in Japan also produced a few 1:24 aircraft, though it was Trumpeter from China who picked up the reins in the early 21st century and started a new line of 1:24 aircraft kits.

1:350

Perhaps the most popular scale for maritime subjects, 1:350 offers a good compromise between smaller vessels and larger ones. Leading the field are Tamiya, Hasegawa, Revell, Trumpeter and Dragon, with Airfix recently joining the fold. There are also specialist companies like White Ensign whose range – while not suitable for, or aimed at, beginners – offers complete resin kits and photo-etched brass accessories for the experienced modeller used to working with those materials.

Fig 2.6 The Spitfire continues to be a popular choice for a first model – this is the PR.XIX kit released in 2009.

1:700

Second only to 1:350 for maritime subjects, and conveniently half the size, 1:700 is equally dominated by the same names as the larger scale – Tamiya, Hasegawa, Dragon, Revell and Trumpeter along with Fujimi.

OTHER SCALES

There are many other scales out there, some of them the result of early kits being scaled to fit a box, and some that came about as a result of the adoption of metric rather than imperial measurements – the metric 1:100 and 1:50 scales being such

examples, as opposed to the imperial 1:96 and 1:48.

French kit manufacturer Heller championed 1:100 and 1:50 in their early years but eventually moved to 1:72 and 1:48, though they doggedly stuck to their own scales of 1:125 and 1:400 that were oddly out of step with the rest of the modelling world.

Revell and Italeri have some ship kits in 1:720, Airfix 1:600 and 1:1200. Certain car kits are available in 1:43, 1:20, 1:18, 1:16 and 1:12 scales.

THE RIGHT STUFF

In choosing any model either as a first kit or as something to hone your skills, it is

Fig 2.7 The Komet's tail – two entry-level kits of the unusual Messerschmitt 163 Komet rocket fighter by Academy (top) and Hobbyboss (bottom).

better to start with something both manageable and affordable, and then build up your experience from there. You will probably learn more from making several smaller, easier projects than trying to tackle one large one. There are a lot of skills involved in making models, many of them instinctive, while others have to be learned. All of them get better with practise. And while rushing to complete a kit never produces a good model, there is a natural impulse to see how a finished model looks – even amongst experienced modellers – and so the easier the project for the beginner, the quicker the results, and, in turn, the greater the likelihood of another model being made to galvanise on the enthusiasm and keep fresh the skills being learned. It's a natural part of the process for a modeller to look back on their early work and think 'I can do better than that' and it's here that other skills like patience and a more methodical approach come into play. If anything, modelling is a constant refinement of skills and techniques – you never stop learning.

As much as it is something of a cliché that many modellers started out making a 1:72 Spitfire, it is also true; for the simple reason that a 1:72 Spitfire (or Hurricane, Bf 109, P-51 Mustang or Mitsubishi Zero) is a more solid choice for a beginner than a 1:72 Lancaster or Flying Fortress. This is simply because there are fewer parts and joins, and the size of the kit pieces are more compact and manageable with, consequently, a

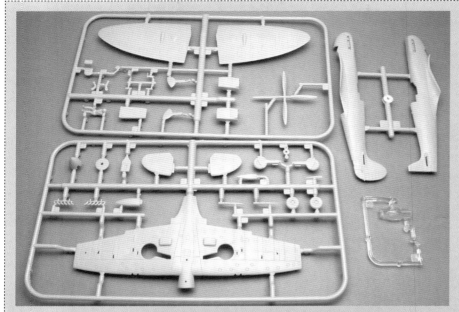

Fig 2.8 The spread of parts for the new Airfix 1:72 Spitfire Mk.IX released in 2009 — a good choice of kit for the less experienced modeller.

smaller surface area to paint, and less expense involved.

As mentioned above, the larger the scale, the larger the model and the likelihood there will be more parts and details to deal with and paint. A 1:24 Spitfire may not be an ideal choice for the novice, not only because of the cost and complexity of the kit, but because the sheer physical size may present a challenge both in terms of construction and painting. While there are some 1:48 subjects that are suitable for beginners (again perhaps the Spitfire,

Hurricane or even modern jets like a Hawk) to get the best results from the larger scales like 1:32 and 1:24 really does require more experience — and that only comes with practise.

Another factor is expense — if you are relatively new to modelling it is better to start out with a more modestly priced kit than a more expensive one, and for the most part the more affordable kits tend to be aimed at the entry-level modeller anyway. Expense is also a consideration if you do accidentally mess something up or it

doesn't turn out as expected; at least your investment will only have been moderate.

Model manufacturers have tried to assist beginners in the past and continue do so to this day. Almost every kit company has, at some stage, produced snap-together kits of cars or aircraft and some offer pre-painted kits that just need basic gluing or snapping together. These can be ideal for really young modellers who would rather skip past the whole painting stage.

Kit companies also offer starter sets or gift sets that include glue, paint and brushes. These are by no means fully comprehensive but offer the bare bones to get started. You may wish to supplement these with other paints or colours — after all, a small pot of Dark Earth paint supplied might be enough for one coat but not two, and many models really demand the latter for a good finish. With standard kits, some manufacturers like Airfix, Revell and Italeri will also list the paints needed to complete specific colour or camouflage schemes. It might seem like a rather large outlay to buy a dozen tins or bottles of paint at first, but properly looked after these will last for many projects and recoup the initial investment.

It will take time and experience to build up a collection of colours, but a selection of basic shades — black, white, yellow, blue, red and silver — can also be used to create custom mixes, thus providing an initial saving. A variety of metallic colours can be

Fig 2.9 : This Revell 1:76 Sd Kfz 234/2 Puma armoured car is a rebox of the Matchbox kit and includes a diorama display base – an ideal kit for the beginner.

Fig 2.10 Another ex-Matchbox kit now reboxed by Revell, this is the sleek Jagdpanzer IV L/70 Lang 'tank-hunter'.

Fig 2.11 This 1:72 P-39 Airacobra by Hobbyboss assembles in minutes thanks to its simplified construction.

created, like for example gunmetal, by simply mixing silver and black; or adonized aluminium by mixing silver and white. Similarly, gloss and matt varnishes widen the scope– you don't need gloss black for small items when you can overpaint gloss varnish to matt black.

AIRCRAFT

As mentioned, you cannot go too far wrong with a Spitfire or almost any kind of single-engined fighter aircraft. The paint schemes tend to be matt, largely easier to paint and more forgiving than, say, the gloss finish needed for an airliner.

Biplanes are perhaps best avoided as even the high quality kits still require careful setting and aligning of the wings and struts, and the finished models can be quite

fragile. There are some exceptions, which are sturdier in design like the Airfix Roland C.II (currently out of production). Biplanes are certainly something to try later, especially as they require mastering new skills like making and adding flying wires, but are perhaps not an ideal choice right at the start.

Some older Airfix kits like the Airfix P-40 Kittyhawk and A-4 Skyhawk – very basic in terms of detail, given their origins, which date from the 1950s and 1960s – have proven to be ideal in the hands of the many youngsters who have taken part in the 'Make and Take' events run by Airfix at model shows and air displays thanks to the small number of parts and robust mouldings.

In recent years Airfix have started to replace some of their older, popular kits with

more modern tooling. Kits like the old Spitfire Mk.IX – known as 'JEJ' by modellers because of its lifelong association with the scheme worn by legendary RAF ace Johnnie Johnson – have been retired in favour of all-new kits that offer greater accuracy and better-fitting parts.

The Revell range features some of the former Matchbox aircraft kits. The low parts count and often simplified construction makes these excellent starter kits now as they were nearly forty years ago when they were first released – admittedly the Matchbox Sea Harrier cannot equal the ESCI (now Italeri) kit for detail and finesse, but equally the ESCI kit cannot equal the Matchbox Sea Harrier for ease of construction.

One ingenious innovation in recent years has been the Hobbyboss range of 'easy build' kits; simplified models that usually comprise of a one piece fuselage that clips onto a wing. This means that models can be constructed literally in minutes and the results can be indistinguishable from the more traditional models. Similarly, Pegasus Models from the USA (not to be confused with the former British cottage company) also produce 1:48 kits on a similar principle.

TANKS AND ARMOUR

For someone looking to break into 1:35 vehicles the choice is wide and potentially problematical – not because there are so many bad kits, quite the opposite; there are many excellent kits, but they often have features, details or options not suitable for a beginner.

The tracks in tank kits, for example, tend to come in two forms, either as one-piece vinyl items that require careful joining or as link-by-link tracks that offer amazing results but are mini-modelling projects in themselves and can tax even the most experienced modellers. Some kits may have photo-etched brass parts for really fine items like mesh screens or light guards, but these require careful removal from sprues, and precise trimming and gluing – something best avoided until you have a few kits under your belt and/or have built up some experience using mixed media materials on simpler projects.

In choosing a 1:35 kit for a beginner, it

Fig 2.12 A 1:72 Dragon Sherman Firefly, showing the intricate photo-etched detail parts included in the box, making this a model for the more experienced modeller.

Fig 2.13 Sailing ships make for attractive, colourful subjects, such as this Airfix *Golden Hind*. Model by Adam Cooper.

is better to stick to a simpler, perhaps smaller project to start out with – a novice should have fewer problems with a Jeep, Universal ('Bren') Carrier or an armoured car than a Tiger or Panther tank. In fact armoured cars do offer the advantage of having fewer wheels to paint and no tracks to worry about!

Some of the older Tamiya 1:35 kits tend to be more simplified (relative to Tamiya's high standards) either with fewer parts or one-piece tracks, so may be more suitable for the beginner. The more recent Tamiya tanks tend to be far more intricate, not to mention expensive. Similarly Dragon's range of 1:35 military kits really is cutting edge stuff, using complicated moulding techniques to produce incredible amounts of detail, but this can result in a high number of parts, mixed media materials and a premium retail price.

In the smaller scales of 1:72 and 1:76 kits, there are some kits that are more suitable than others – the Airfix Sherman tank is more manageable for a beginner than their Churchill, which at over 100 parts, has a lot of small wheels on the running gear to contend with (Matchbox and ESCI subsequently found better ways to reproduce this). Some of the old JB Models kits – now reboxed by Airfix – are good kits for the newcomer, being both simple and affordable. The Revell range also includes many of the old 1:76 Matchbox armour kits that come with the added bonus of a

Fig 2.14 Japan's love affair with that most British of icons, the Mini, extends to their model industry as well. This 1:24 Tamiya kit depicts the classic Cooper S model.

diorama base for display purposes, and these make excellent kits for the beginner.

At the really basic level there are simplified kits made by Armourfast and Italeri that are aimed at wargamers but which are capable of being made up into fine looking models – these are good canvas on which to practice your skills, especially for those modellers with limited time to devote to the hobby.

The flip side is Dragon's range of 1:72 armour, which offers really superb models for the discerning enthusiast, but they can also sometimes include photo-etched or white metal parts, not to mention some very delicate plastic mouldings for the scale – often incredible kits, but ones that require patience and experience.

Figure modellers in 1:35 also have a wide choice, Tamiya and Dragon again dominating the field though it may be better to start out with painting simpler uniforms like German field grey or British khaki than the more complicated WWII or modern day camouflage patterns. If figure painting is something you fancy practising then you can't go much wrong with the current range of 1:32 Airfix figures that require no assembly.

SHIPS

Ship models can be, perhaps, amongst the more complicated kits to make, either because of the number of parts, their delicacy or the amount of painting and subassemblies needed. A novice modeller who decides to tackle an aircraft carrier will certainly get their money's worth, not least painting all the aircraft that sit on the flight deck, but it may be a project too far at an early stage. Similarly, something like a 1:350 *Bismarck* or *Tirpitz*, as fine as those kits are, cannot be rushed and require a certain amount of pre-painting to get the best out of them.

Again, the smaller scales and smaller subjects tend to make for better choices. In fact there's very little can go wrong with a submarine – they're mostly devoid of fine details, require fewer colours and can be made as full hull or waterline models. Similarly, a small frigate or destroyer model is going to be more manageable than a battleship or carrier.

If military subjects don't appeal then there are merchant ships and ocean liners available from various manufacturers. Sailing ships, while very attractive subjects, can also be demanding, especially with the rigging that many require, not to mention all the deck fittings and detail painting.

CARS

In terms of subject matter, it again comes down to scale and price – the 1:32

Airfix Bentley 'blower' is much easier to make and paint than the 1:12 version. Again, the larger the scale, the more complex the kit is likely to be, not to mention more expensive.

Many American kit companies like AMT and Monogram make 'kerbside' models that have simpler chassis and engine details, and being at either 1:24 or 1:25 scale, are a good manageable size too, ideal for the beginner.

Perhaps the only real pitfalls with car kits for the beginner ie not in the actual construction, but in getting a good paint finish. Experienced car modellers use the same paints, tools and techniques as real automotive finishers, and it's an often laborious process to get that perfect, showroom finish.

Getting a good painted finish on the bodyshell of a car model really does require the use of either spray cans or an airbrush; skills that certainly can be mastered, but only over time and with considerable practise to get right. That's not to say a novice might not get good results with their first attempt with a spray can, and many do, but it does require care – and we'll be looking at using cans in a later chapter.

The alternative for the beginner is simply not to paint the bodyshell at all and just polish the natural plastic colour – while enthusiasts may wince at the idea, it does offer a convenient route to a smooth, shiny finish.

Fig 2.15 The untreated joins, bare plastic, gaps, poorly mixed and applied paint, glue smears and crooked decals are an example of how not to make a model!

Subjects like rally cars can allow the modeller to indulge in weathering effects, so a less than perfect paint finish can be disguised under layers of dust and mud. About the only downside of rally cars, and racing cars like Formula 1 cars or dragsters, can be the large number of sponsor's logo decals that typically need to be applied.

RESEARCH

Strictly speaking there is no reason why anyone cannot or should not make a model as directed by the construction and finishing diagrams, in fact many do just that, but at some stage almost every modeller who has made a few kits starts to look for something different to do, to put their own personal stamp on a model. They may have read or seen an article, a book or film about a particular subject and wondered how they could reproduce that in kit form. It might be something as simple as basic weathering or a change of colour scheme and markings, to adding rigging or flags to a ship, additional stowage to a tank, or cockpit details to an aeroplane. Or it may be rather involved, perhaps a conversion to a different variant, either adding a new propeller or turret, or removing a section of fuselage or the upper decking of a tank, altering the guns on a ship, or lowering the suspension of a car. This is where the researching aspect of the hobby comes in.

Perhaps the first introduction to researching comes when a modeller looks for different colour schemes that differ to those illustrated in the kit instructions. Most kits are supplied with decals, sometimes of variants or colour schemes that may not be well-known, thus prompting some research to learn more about them. Most people are familiar with the role of the Hawker Hurricane with the RAF in the Battle of Britain, but what about the Hurricanes in service with Irish Air Corps? Or what about the Messerschmitt Bf109E, familiar to everyone in its Luftwaffe guise, but in the Romanian Air Force? Small seeds like that can fire the imagination and lead even budding newcomers to want to learn more about the subject matter; the historical information behind the kit they are making.

Fig 2.16 Now in its fourth decade, *Tamiya's Model Magazine International* showcases some of the best modelling around.

Fig 2.17 Launched in Novermber 2010, *Airfix Model World* is the latest magazine to hit the scene.

Fig 2.18 *Model Military International* magazine showcases some of the finest military modelling around.

Fig 2.19 Osprey's *Aircraft of the Aces* series combine detailed historical accounts with photographs and colour illustrations.

Fig 2.20 The Squadron Signal *In Action* books have long been the staple of many modellers' reference libraries.

Research can also help in correcting any faults or errors in a kit. While the levels of accuracy have improved over the years as more information and technology has become available, sometimes kit companies can get things wrong. Some mistakes can be minor, requiring some simple sanding, reshaping or conversion work to correct; others can be major, necessitating a lot of effort – and in rare instances it might be so involved as to be near impossible. In such cases compromises will of course have to be made.

Perhaps unsurprisingly it is older kits that sometimes have more accuracy problems. A famous example in the Airfix range is the 1:76 Sf Kfz 234/2 armoured car, which comes with a set of incorrect shorter, individual mudguards when some basic research will show that what it really needs are the longer, continuous examples similar to those fitted to the Sd Kfz 234/2 Puma.

The fault may not be down to the makers of the kit. Airfix's 1:72 Fairey Battle was based on original Fairey drawings and was tooled up exactly as specified – the problem was that Fairey supplied Airfix with the wrong drawings and the kit ended up faithfully depicting an early development design rather than the actual production aircraft.

Conversely there are kits that are totally correct, but they depict a defunct variant that never saw service. The 1:72 Airfix Handley Page Jetstream kit (currently out of production) depicts the C-10A version intended for the United States Air Force but which was cancelled around the same time Airfix released their kit. Simple research will show that, alas, it has the wrong engines for the Royal Air Force and Royal Navy versions, as well some important fuselage differences.

The 1:600 HMS *Campbeltown* kit needs some work to accurately depict her March 1942 configuration when she took part in the famous raid on St Nazaire. In fact ships often change during refits and with a little research you can soon discover both subtle and obvious differences to the guns, masts, colour schemes etc.

Ultimately the amount of research you undertake depends on what you wish to get out of your modelling, the resources available, and the importance you personally attach to faithful historical reproduction.

BOOKS AND MAGAZINES

The range of books and magazines available is equally as staggering as the number of kits, with volumes large and small covering every subject imaginable from their histories to colour schemes and markings.

For the modeller there are newsstand magazines like S*cale Aircraft Modelling*, *Scale Aviation Modeller*, *Scale Models*, *Model Aircraft Monthly*, *Model Aircraft Magazine*, *Military Modelling*, *Military Modelworld*, *Tamiya Magazine* and *Airfix Model World* in the UK, *Fine Scale Modeler* and *Scale Auto Magazine* in the USA. For the most part these mix historical background articles with modelling features and reviews. For the aviation enthusiast there are long running titles like *Aeroplane*, *Air Forces Monthly* and *Flypast*.

In the field of books, Osprey have led the way for many years with their 'Vanguard', 'Men-at-Arms' and 'Aircraft of the Aces' series that feature lots of photographs and a set of colour illustrations. Osprey have also ventured into modelling titles covering specific subjects utilising cutting edge techniques and products.

Squadron's 'In Action' series from the USA are good primers on aircraft, military and maritime subjects, while the 'Detail and Scale' range focuses more on close up and interior photos, scale plans and detailed kit reviews. The fall of the Iron Curtain has seen a surge of high quality books on former Eastern Bloc aircraft, tanks, ships and uniforms.

There are also many older, out of production books that are worth seeking out like the 'Profile' series from the 1960s, the 'Camouflage and Markings' booklets published by Ducimus and the 'Aeroguide' books from the 1980s. Bargain bookstores and charity shops can often yield good references at low prices.

Local libraries are an often forgotten source of information; a keyword search through their catalogues can help in finding particular titles, sometimes yielding books that are out of print. Almost all libraries can order books in from other branches, usually for a very modest fee, if not free.

Perhaps the best source these days for researching is the Internet. If you require interior photos of a Spitfire, uniform details of the Africa Korps or a photographic walk-around of a Sherman tank, these are easy to find with the click of a button, and if you cannot find that piece of information you are looking for there are almost always people who can help you on the myriad of modelling forums and web sites out there – a list of useful resources is published at the end of this book.

Finally there are the reference sources you start to build up yourself. Trips to museums, bases, events and air shows are excellent opportunities to create your own photographic library – seeing a subject first hand can also aid in building a greater understanding. Digital cameras are capable of taking thousands of images at high resolution all of which can be stored on a single disc, CD or DVD – the equivalent to hundreds of filing cabinets full of photographic prints! A simple scrapbook for any press cuttings or magazine articles you come across can also be a good method of gathering information.

Fig 2.21 and **Fig 2.22** Air and military vehicle shows are an excellent opportunity to take detailed photographs of subjects, like this Dodge 4x4 or Harrier jet.

A. Tooby

HOW ARE KITS MADE?

For many years the process of making a model kit could take two years or more and was a labour intensive task involving researchers, designers and pattern makers. General arrangement and component drawings would be prepared for craftsmen to make all the parts – or patterns – out of wood or metal. These were usually more than twice the size of the finished part and would be used as a guide to cut the mould to actual scale using a 3D tracing tool called a pantograph – slow and meticulous work, not to mention expensive. Test shots would then be produced and any minor adjustments would be made to make the kit mould properly. Artwork for the instruction sheets and decals were hand drawn, the final layouts pasted up then converted to film separations for printing using a reprographics camera.

These days the process has been revolutionised through the use of CAD – Computer Aided Design. In fact almost every aspect of how Airfix make their kits is now produced on computers, from the kit design to box art, packaging and decals.

The decision making that goes into selecting a new Airfix kit is a very thorough process and various factors come into play in whittling down the choices. Perhaps the prime factor is sales – it is sometimes better to have 15% of a market for something that sells, than 100% of a market for something that doesn't. Another consideration is the need to replace older tooling, and since 2008 Airfix has begun to retire some of its best selling, albeit older kits in favour of new-tooled versions that are more in line with the standards expected today. A look through the history of the aircraft kits that Airfix have made over the years shows that two of the most popular subjects are Spitfires and Harriers – and with good reason, as they're probably the two most famous and recognisable aircraft in the UK, if not the world. Other 'evergreen' subjects include the Hurricane, Bf 109, Mosquito and Lancaster.

Export sales are also an important factor. In the past Airfix have released special boxings of kits for specific markets, Sweden being one such example. Similarly a strong overseas market may dictate the inclusion of an additional decal scheme. The number of variations that can be wrung from a kit are also examined, either as optional parts included in a kit or held over for possible future releases, all of which affects the number of parts and possible price point of the kit.

The research phase begins with gathering as much information as possible from photographs, books, magazines and original manufacturers drawings and data. Where practical, full size examples are photographed and extensively measured, either in museums or at airfields, naval stations or army bases, depending on the subject – the 2009 new-tool Airfix Hawk kits were based on BAE Systems own CAD models, the 1:48 Seafire XVII was measured from the aircraft at the Fleet Air Arm Museum at RNAS Yeovilton, while the Trafalgar Class Submarine and HMS *Illustrious* were designed with the full co-operation of the Royal Navy who allowed first hand access.

Sometimes research can overturn some long held beliefs or myths that have become established as 'fact' over the years – for example some published works stated that the undercarriage track of the Seafire 46/47 was wider than that of the equivalent Spitfire 22/24, but research using original Supermarine documents and photos showed that they were in fact exactly the same.

DESIGN

With all the reference material to hand, the actual CAD design can begin, and this is a meticulous process as the various measurements are translated into drawings and shapes which are constantly refined. CAD also allows the breakdown of the parts to be determined at this stage and the model 'virtually' assembled on screen. Moulding considerations are also worked out at this stage, like the layout of parts, positioning of gates and runners (the channels molten plastic flows through to reach the part) and draft angles (where the details on curved surfaces need to be moulded evenly), all of which can be interdependent factors.

While scale fidelity is always the ultimate aim, sometimes moulding something to absolute scale may be impossible or impractical, either because they would be too small or thin to reproduce properly. Missile and bomb fins are usually only a few millimetres thick in real life – and would be conspicuous by their absence if left off. But they could not be reproduced 100% to scale in 1:72 or 1:48, so they have to be designed slightly thicker than normal so they can be moulded.

With the CAD designs finalised the information is sent off for rapid prototyping, a process where a model is produced by the Stereolithographic (SLA) process using a laser to build each part from a liquid of photopolymer resin. While not as refined as the actual injection moulding process itself, the SLA model gives the designers a chance to assess their work as a physically three dimensional form and to further refine the shape or fit of the parts.

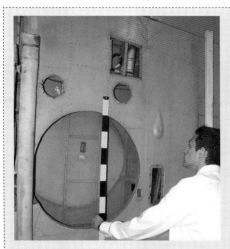

Fig 3.1 One of the Airfix design team measuring the wheel well of a Spitfire.

Fig 3.2 An oil cooler for a Spitfire being measured.

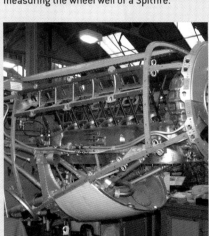

Fig 3.3 Access to the actual subject offers the chance to record every detail accurately.

Fig 3.4 This Spitfire at the Imperial War Museum, London, shows details on the underside that are usually harder to access with a 'parked' machine.

Fig 3.5 The 1:24 Mosquito is perhaps the most complex kit Airfix have ever made, with over 600 parts and decals for four schemes.

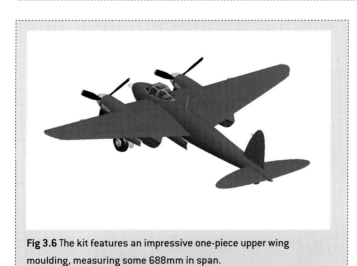

Fig 3.6 The kit features an impressive one-piece upper wing moulding, measuring some 688mm in span.

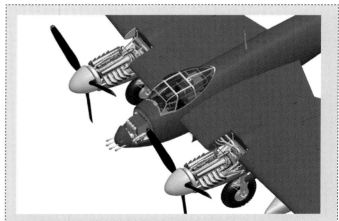

Fig 3.7 This Computer Aided Design (CAD) image shows the detail for the engines and the nose armament.

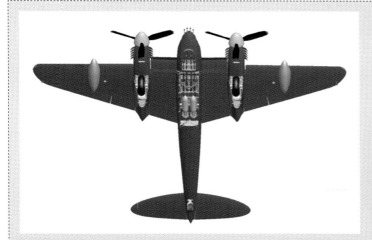

Fig 3.8 The kit also features a fully equipped bomb bay as well as external drop tanks.

Fig 3.9 The cockpit detail is complete and even includes pre-printed dial faces for the instrument panel.

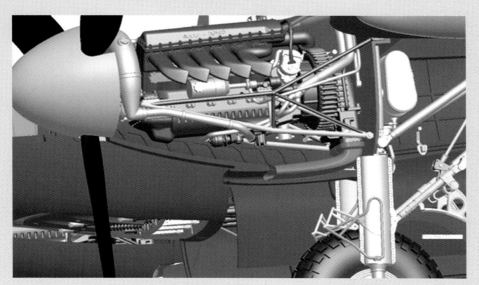

Fig 3.10 A close up of one of the highly detailed Merlin engines, almost a modelling project in themselves.

Fig 3.11 Once back in the design studio the construction of the model can begin using Computer Aided Design (CAD). Here a test shot is being compared to the original CAD data.

Fig 3.12 An injection moulding machine, capable of turning out hundreds of models an hour.

Once the CAD work has been finished the data can then be uploaded – in a matter of minutes – to the mould makers, either in China or India and preparations made to start cutting the steel for the actual moulds. This can take upwards of several months and results in test shots which are then meticulously checked over to make sure the data has been accurately translated and that all the parts fit as intended. Any minor changes can be made, and checked before the kit is ready for production.

Moulds tend to be made from hardened steel and come in two halves, held together with steel pins – these have to be strong because the moulds are subject to great pressures during the moulding process. The durability of steel moulds can be measured by the fact that some Airfix moulds created over 50 years ago are still in production, perhaps longer than their original designers ever imagined or intended! A relatively recent innovation in model manufacture is slide moulding, when a part is made up of several moulds that interlock with each other. Slide moulding enables complex parts and details to be made that would be impossible to do with conventional two-part moulds.

Modern injection moulding systems use thermoplastics that are fed into the moulding machine in a granulated form, heated and then injected into the mould. Water-cooling systems ensure that the machines run at the right temperature enabling the plastic parts to cool and become rigid within seconds before being ejected from the mould fairly rapidly. On average the moulding cycle is capable of producing 100 kits an hour (depending on the number of sprues per kit) meaning an initial run of thousands of kits can be completed in a day or so.

DECALS

The research for the box art and decal schemes is carried out in tandem. A balance is usually struck between something that is historically interesting or important with a scheme that is either attractive or unusual. The 2010 reissue of the 1:72 Hurricane Mk.I kit is a good example, mixing markings for a Battle of Britain era aircraft to mark the 70th anniversary of that famous conflict with a more unusual secondary option in the form of an Irish Air Corps machine.

The decal design process closely mirrors that of the actual kit design with the same meticulous research-gathering process. Where possible the original diagrams used to paint and mark full size subjects – for example a Eurofighter Typhoon – are sought, or visits to museums and bases take place and every marking from the roundels to the smallest stencilling is meticulously measured, recorded and photographed. In the case of older, historical subjects, it's a matter of consulting authoritative sources or studying hundreds of photographs to decipher information.

There have been instances of aircraft restorers contacting Airfix for help with colour schemes and markings for the aircraft they are working on – the Royal Navy Historic Flight's Seahawk benefited from research being done by Dick Ward of Modeldecal who was creating decals for Airfix's 1:72 RNHF Seahawk, while one restoration team working on a Spitfire used a CD of decal designs intended for an Airfix kit to create templates for their own markings.

Decal designs are often drawn 1:1 on a computer; this ensures absolutely accuracy,

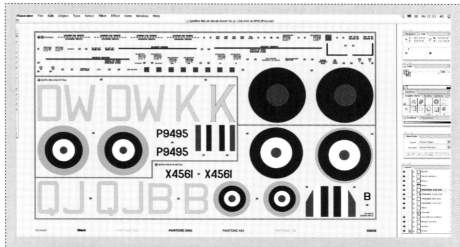

Fig 3.13 The decal sheet is also designed on computer, markings are drawn 1:1 and then scaled down to the required size.

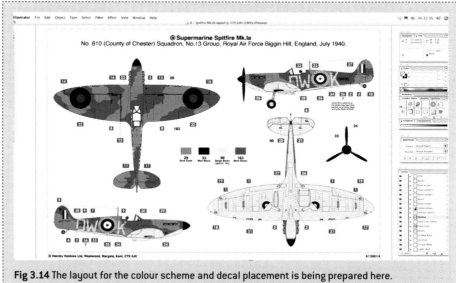

Fig 3.14 The layout for the colour scheme and decal placement is being prepared here.

especially when it comes to roundels, code letters and serial numbers that are then scaled-down to the required size. Test shots are used to check that specific items fit the kit, like the liveries on an airliner when items have to be shaped so that they look right e.g. a fuselage cheat line that goes over a curved surface. Colour traps – where a lighter colour is printed fractionally larger so that the subsequent darker colour 'traps' it underneath to prevent any gaps (for example the blue and yellow on an RAF roundel) – are also worked out and the finished artwork is then proofed and, once approved, uploaded to the printers who then output the artwork as film separations ready for making up into screens for printing. The decals are printed onto a special paper containing a layer of water-soluble glue. The layering process starts with the lightest colours through to the darkest, the paper being stored in temperature and humidity-controlled conditions between runs to stop it expanding or contracting (which would affect the registration of colours). Finally the varnish layer is applied – without which, the inks would disintegrate – and the sheets then trimmed ready for dispatch.

The colour scheme and decal placement diagrams are also finalised and uploaded to the printers, either for incorporation onto the packaging or to be slotted into the construction sequence booklet.

BOX ART

Since 2008 Airfix have employed cutting edge Computer Generated Imagery (CGI) for most of its new box art, mostly produced by Adam Tooby. Typically the CGI artwork takes around five to six days and starts with a wire frame model based on general arrangement drawings. This is then 'skinned' and surface detail added to produce 'clays' – basic grey renderings used to check the shapes are accurate. CGI allows the artist to position the virtual 'clay' models and render various 'roughs' to try out various angles and compositions that work best within the shape of the packaging – not unlike the pencil roughs that former Airfix artist Roy Cross would have submitted in the past. With the composition agreed upon Adam can then add the colour schemes and markings, working closely alongside the decal designer to assure that everything matches as closely as possible. There then follows the process of adding skies, backgrounds, effects, motion blur and atmospherics before 'lighting' the model and producing a full render – a process that takes a lot of computing power and which can last several hours even with powerful computers.

The amount of research that goes into the box art is perhaps best illustrated by the 1:24 Mosquito, which depicts the famous Operation Jericho raid on the prison at Amiens, Belgium. Aside from the details of the aircraft schemes, recourse to first-hand accounts by the aircrew, archive film and photographs of the raid and Met Office reports of the weather were also consulted. The attack took place in winter and the prison was heavily blanketed by snow so the topography of the area was carefully studied to put the aircraft on the right approach to the prison and even the angle and position of the sun at the time of the raid was researched to ensure that the lighting conditions could be replicated within the computer. The 1:24 Mosquito artwork is regarded as one of the modern day classics on a par with some of the great Roy Cross paintings like 'G for George'.

With all the box art elements completed, the packaging designs can be finalised, adding details like the number of parts and paint codes specific to the kit, before the box art and side profiles are dropped in. With the arrival of the plastic parts all the various elements can now be brought together and the kits packed up ready for distribution.

Fig 3.15 The CG wireframe Spitfire model has been 'wrapped' in the final colour scheme and rendered, while the positions of other aircraft have also been sketched in.

Fig 3.16 The landscape, also computer generated, has been added at this stage, along with atmospheric effects to provide haze on the horizon.

Fig 3.17 A Junkers Ju 88 has been added and rendered, replacing the rough positional. A nice touch is the starboard undercarriage leg partly down.

Fig 3.18 A second Ju 88 and Spitfire are also added, and the artwork begins to tell a story of a formation being 'bounced' by the RAF.

Fig 3.19 The rest of the formation of Ju 88s can now be added and carefully lit and rendered to create the impression of depth and atmosphere.

Fig 3.20 A final touch are the vapour trails in the distance and the composition is completed ready to be dropped into the packaging artwork.

TOOLS FOR THE JOB

The 21st century modeller really is spoiled for choice when it comes to the quantity and quality of tools available. It would be very easy for a newcomer to walk out of a model shop having spent more than they expected on all kinds of tools, equipment and paint they may never need, often eagerly recommended by some well meaning enthusiasts hoping to get them off to the right start. But like all hobbies you grow into the things you need as your skills, confidence and interests progress.

A modelling tool kit (excluding paints) for a beginner can be broken down to (A) the basics that you will need to get started, (B) the additional items that you may need as your skills, experience and ambitions progress and (C) general everyday items that will have their uses.

But to get started you simply need the following tools:

- Cutting mat
- Cutters
- Knife
- Sanding sticks
- Glue
- Tweezers

Fig 4.1 A selection of basic tools needed to get started on a model – side cutters, knife, sanding stick, tweezers and glue.

Cutting mat Essential to protect adjacent surfaces from damage by knives, paint etc. Cutting mats used to be the preserve of graphic design studios and were relatively expensive, but these days A5 mats can be found in discount stores for next to nothing. Almost all cutting mats feature a useful grid for measuring, especially when it comes to cutting masking tape in straight lines. If you can't get hold of a cutting mat then almost any suitable piece of wood or hardboard can be turned into a modelling work surface, though as an extra precaution lay down some old newspaper underneath it to protect underlying surfaces.

Cutters The easiest and safest way of removing parts from the sprue – especially if the sprue gates are thick – is to use a pair of cutters and these can be had cheaply,

Fig 4.2 Some of the commercially available modelling glues showing tube, needle and liquid types.

though there are also some made specially for modellers. Many people use these in conjunction with a knife, the cutters being used to remove the parts and the knife to clean up any remaining plastic.

A modelling knife Essential for removing, trimming and tidying up parts, anything from a good old Stanley knife to craft knives with the break-off blades and surgical scalpels have their uses. A modelling knife with interchangeable blades is a good start, and while there are cheaper varieties out there to be had in bargain stores, it's worth investing in a good quality product like X-Acto or Swann Morton – next to glue it's the one thing you'll be using the most so it's worth going for quality. A variety of blades is also an excellent investment, not least because it's always handy to have spares. A curved blade is good for very general model-

ling work, but a pointed blade allows more finesse, especially when dealing with small parts or cutting masking tape. Experienced modellers sometimes have a variety of knives with different blades in their toolbox, each one reserved for a specific task (e.g. a heavy duty blade for cutting, a scalpel for trimming, one for clear parts etc.).

It goes without saying that knives are sharp and should be treated with the utmost respect and caution. Always store them away safely and wrap any broken or blunt blades in tape before disposing of them responsibly. As a general guide a good quality blade will last one kit, maybe two at most, but beyond that trying to use a blunt or worn blade will not only start damaging parts as you try to remove or trim them, but will increase the risk of a serious accident, either by breaking or slipping.

Glue Decades back the most widely available kind of modelling glue was tube glue, a solvent suspended in a gelatinous, stringy carrier. You may still come across these, but they are best avoided as they can be messy. Most modern glues come either in a bottle as a liquid cement applied with a brush or a slight thicker kind with a metal needle applicator.

Although known as 'glue' or 'plastic cement', most modern day glues are actually a solvent that chemically welds the plastic together by melting it – it goes

without saying that using too much can lead to disaster!

Some bottles of liquid cement come with a small brush attached to the cap, for others (like EMA Plastic Weld) you will need one – a cheap artist's paintbrush is ideal, or you can buy proprietary modellers brushes sold for this task.

Suffice to say that extreme care is needed while using modelling glues – read the safety label and NEVER intentionally breathe in the vapours or ingest any types of glues, as they are often toxic. Liquid cements are designed to evaporate fast so always close the lid when not in use, even if it is just for a few minutes in-between gluing parts.

Sanding sticks Similar in appearance to emery boards used by beauticians, sanding sticks are made of an abrasive material bonded to foam backing. Unlike emery boards, which tend to be just a bit of sandpaper glued on a piece of card or thin wood and thus rather rigid, sanding sticks are more flexible and so don't produce 'flat spots' when sanding down the join between, for example, two fuselage halves. Sanding sticks also come in a variety of grits, the higher the number the finer the grit, so you can use a coarse one for sanding down difficult seams or areas of filler, and a finer one for finishing off the join and smoothing down the plastic. Most can also be used wet, with a dash of washing up

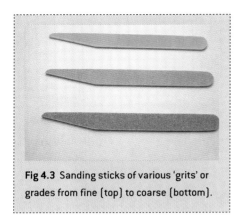

Fig 4.3 Sanding sticks of various 'grits' or grades from fine (top) to coarse (bottom).

liquid, which helps lubricate the grit and stop it from clogging, especially when sanding down large areas of filler.

Some beauty stores and discount shops stock foam-backed sticks for polishing and buffing nails which are very similar to the modelling ones and can usually be bought very cheaply. These can be very useful in polishing clear parts that may be damaged or need reshaping, so it is worth getting a pack as an addition to your toolbox.

Tweezers Ideal for holding and installing small parts, you can buy tweezers of all shapes and size, either pointed or blunt. A basic set of eyebrow tweezers from a beauty shop or pharmacists are enough to get you started – these are compact and offer good control. Some cheap tweezers may not align at the tip properly or the metal can be very soft and prone to

bending, so it's worth shopping around for a decent pair. Some form of grooved tips are preferable as they can grip parts and prevent them from flying out of your grasp. A good investment is a pair of self-locking tweezers that hold parts under tension, especially as you can put these down with the part still held in place, ideal when painting items.

Those are the basics but what other tools and equipment can be useful for your modelling workbench?

Other glues Once your modelling skills progress you may find the need to use other types of glue to bond dissimilar materials, like metal, wood or resin to plastic. For this you can either use the eponymous 'Superglue' that bonds instantly or a two-part epoxy adhesive. Superglue comes in either a runny liquid form or as a gel. The latter is better in inexperienced hands as there is less chance of accidents, though care still has to be exercised as it bonds skin instantly – in fact its origins stem from just that purpose for medical uses. Commercial 'debonders' can help if you get stuck (literally). Conversely there are also 'accelerators', liquids that produce a chemical reaction that sets superglue almost instantaneously. Some modellers like to use superglue as filler in conjunction with an accelerator, the glue will dry as hard as plastic – in fact over time harder than plastic – and can be sanded and polished to a

smooth finish but it is very much an advanced technique and best avoided by the beginner getting to grips with modelling, especially when there are actual model fillers available for the task.

Epoxy adhesives come in two parts – the glue itself and the hardener. These can be messy to prepare and use, and they have to be mixed in equal parts, but their slow drying time does enable some adjustment before they set, and the final bond is very strong.

White glue or PVA (Polyvinyl Acetate), used for crafting or woodworking, is very useful for applying clear parts to kits as it will not mark or mar the plastic and any excess can be removed with a damp cloth. Because PVA dries clear it can also fill any slight gaps around the edges of, say, a windscreen on an aircraft or car, and can be useful for making small windows or portholes, or for glazing headlamps or instrument panels – you can even mix it with water based paints to make formation lights on aircraft or vision slits on tanks. Kristal Klear, made by Microscale in the USA, is very similar and works on the same principles.

Filler Even the best modern day kits may sometimes have imperfections, either parts that do not quite match, resulting in slight gaps, or sink marks where the cooling plastic in the mould shrinks, leaving a slight dimple on the surface. For this you will need filler or putty. The most well known brands of filler out there are Humbrol, Revell, Squadron (Greenstuff and Whitestuff) and Milliput.

The Humbrol, Revell and Squadron fillers are solvent-based so they will eat into the plastic to get a 'grip' – use too much and they can melt plastic. These are best applied sparingly, allowed to dry thoroughly (overnight is best) and then sanded down.

Milliput is a water-based two-part epoxy filler that comes as two 'sausages', you simply pick off two equal chunks, knead and mix them together like dough until it is soft and then use – it dries rock hard in a few hours. Milliput can also be worked wet, almost like clay, especially useful when it comes to major reshaping. Water-based fillers can be applied to small gaps – say between a wing and fuselage – and the excess removed with a damp cloth or cotton bud, usually needing no further filling. Vallejo from Spain also make a water-based filler available with a pointed nozzle, ideal for precise application to small areas.

For the advanced modeller there are all kinds of exotic products from Japan like 'Mr Dissolved Putty' which as the name suggests is a syrup-like filler in a bottle and 'Mr Surfacer', a thickish paint/filler that can be used as a primer on surfaces but which can also be used to fill slight gaps. Both products can be applied and the excess removed using isopropyl alcohol (sold at electronics stores).

Cocktail sticks For all the great new tools and accessories that modellers buy and use, the ubiquitous cocktail stick remains the staple of almost every tool box, for either stirring paint, mounting parts like wheels for painting, applying fillers or glues etc.

Files The good old-fashioned modelling file seems to have fallen out of fashion with plastic modellers in recent years, though when it comes to cleaning up metal parts they are still the best tools for the job. A selection is always useful to have around, even if they are limited to just a flat, semi-circular and round file.

Flexi-File Essentially a U-shaped metal handle with a strip of abrasive looped at the ends. The shape of the Flexi-File allows the abrasive to flex when sanding, enabling it to follow the contours of kit parts, especially useful for areas that may be difficult to access with a sanding stick.

Drills An excellent tool for doing very fine drilling work on models like hollowing out gun barrels, portholes and windows, exhaust pipes etc. A hand chuck and a selection of drills is all that is required for really basic modelling work, while at the other end there are electric or battery operated drills which come with a selection of bits from drilling to grinding, cutting and polishing, but these are really for the more experienced modeller.

Fig 4.4 This carburettor intake from a Spitfire suffers a sink mark on the end.

Fig 4.5 This is easily fixed using filler which is then sanded smooth.

Fig 4.6 Model fillers are ideal for plugging gaps or sink marks.

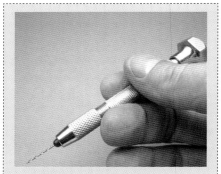

Fig 4.7 A hand held drill is excellent for hollowing out gun barrels or exhaust pipes.

Berna clamps A relatively recent innovation in the modelling world, these are adjustable plastic clamps that can hold items together very firmly but without damaging them.

Razor Saw A handy mini-saw that fits into a knife handle like the X-acto and is ideal for conversion work, like sawing the nose off an aeroplane, the waterline hull of a ship or the decking of a tank.

Masking tape Almost any kind of tape from Sellotape to Magic tape can be utilised, either to bind parts together while waiting for glue to dry, to masking out areas in preparation for painting. Household masking tape – which tends to be a creamy yellow colour – is more flexible than Sellotape and can be made to conform to curved surfaces, though the adhesive can sometimes be too strong and lift paint. Perhaps the best masking

tape for modelling is made by Tamiya. It is low-tack, cuts cleanly and is very flexible – a roll of this would be a good investment.

Blu-Tack Not only a useful item for holding parts or weighting the noses down on some models, Blu-Tack can also be used as a method of masking out camouflage colours when airbrushing, resulting in very fine sprayed edges.

Stretched sprue Not a product you can actually buy (well, almost!) but an old modeller's trick to make fine plastic filaments using the unwanted sprue of a kit. Essentially it involves heating a piece of sprue over a candle until the plastic starts to melt and sag and then gently pulling it apart so that the plastic forms a very thin 'string'. It takes a bit of practise: either the sprue cools too quickly and breaks when being pulled

apart or it's too hot and sags under its own (minute) weight, and even the most experienced modellers need a few tries before they get it right. Once mastered it's an excellent method of making aerials, rigging wires, radar masts etc. but extreme care has to be taken as plastic is very flammable and can give off a toxic black smoke if it actually catches fire. It also goes without saying that molten plastic is very hot and should be allowed to cool before handling. Tea lights are perhaps better to use than conventional candles as they are more stable and less prone to being accidentally knocked over.

RETHINK AND RECYCLE

Modellers are nothing if not resourceful and there are many household and day-to-day items that may lend themselves to modelling in one form or another – jam jars are ideal for storing brushes or for storing white spirit or water for cleaning brushes, while the lids make excellent palettes for mixing paints or applying filler. Old plastic yoghurt pots for can be recycled for mixing paints while some larger, watertight containers (e.g. for takeaways) are great for holding water when applying decals, or in the case of those with lids, even storing spare parts.

Clothes pegs are excellent either for clamping or holding parts. Double-sided tape or sticky foam pads are good for mounting parts onto card for painting. Scotchbrite, a kind of plastic wire-wool abrasive (familiar to most people on washing up scourers) is excellent for polishing down seams after sanding them, preparing a surface for painting, or smoothing down coats of paint. Similarly, many car accessory stores sell abrasive finishing pads that come in a variety of grits that can be used for modelling.

Tippex-type correction fluid can be used for small filling jobs, while some acrylic floor polishes (Future and Pledge) are favoured as high gloss varnishes. Fuse wire makes ideal brake lines and ignition leads, and some types of thread can simulate tow cables.

CD and DVD cleaning sets can yield liquid plastic polish and cloths, even make-up brushes and applicators can prove very useful. Some make-up powders can also be used as pigments for weathering and groundwork. Big make-up blusher brushes are ideal for dusting models.

Old paintbrushes, from the smallest 000 to a large emulsion brush, can be cut up and the bristles used for whip aerials on tanks and aircraft, or dried grass in dioramas. An old toothbrush is excellent for removing dust from panel lines or generally cleaning a model prior to painting.

Unwanted expanded foam packaging can be used as a convenient holder for painting parts or setting them aside as they are drying.

Finally you'll need something to store your modelling tools and paints when not in use, particularly knives and solvents which require safe storage away from youngsters. Many bargain shops sell little plastic toolboxes that are perfect for this purpose, some even include a separate top tray that is ideal for sanding sticks, files or brushes.

WORKSPACE

Many modellers dream of having their own dedicated modelling room with a workbench, paint racks, etc. – somewhere where they can work without having to pack everything away at the end of a session. For many though, modelling has to fit into or around the domestic environment, and as things like paints and glue need care in relation to household furniture, people and pets it is worth following some basic precautions.

As mentioned previously, you'll need something to work on, either a cutting mat or an off-cut of wood. If you are modelling on the dining room or kitchen table, take care to protect this with some layers of old newspaper, or even a black plastic bin liner which will not only catch any dust or plastic shavings but also helps prevent accidental spills from marring domestic surfaces. Always try and make sure any work area is well ventilated.

You'll need light, and plenty of it. Working in daylight is preferable, especially when it comes to painting – some modellers have learned the hard way that paints mixed and applied in artificial light do not always

Fig 4.8 The process of making heat stretched sprue, useful for aircraft rigging wires and aerials. The plastic is held over a candle flame taking care not to let it burn.

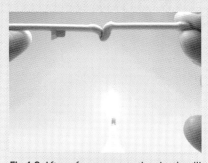

Fig 4.9 After a few moments the plastic will start to go glossy and begin to sag.

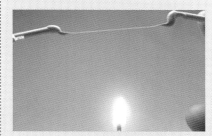

Fig 4.10 The plastic is gently pulled apart resulting in a very fine filament.

look the same in daylight! If you cannot work in daylight – and many people can't, especially in the winter months in the Northern Hemisphere – then a good lamp fitted with a 60 or (preferably) 100-watt bulb in addition to the ambient room lighting is a bonus. At the other end of the spectrum there are specialist hobby lamps that come with magnifying lenses and daylight simulation bulbs. Working in poor light can result in eye strain and headaches, so if a lot of your modelling is being done without the benefit of daylight then it is worth investing in a decent light source.

ANATOMY OF A KIT

Almost every model kit consists of the plastic parts, instructions and a sheet of decals (or transfers) for the markings. Some of the more expensive and complex kits may include a fret of photo-etched, cast resin and/or white metal parts.

The plastic parts are attached to a frame, generally called a sprue, although strictly speaking this only really refers to the small attachments points of the kit parts themselves. The rest are actually runners, the channels through which the molten plastic flows when the kit is being moulded.

Almost every component in a kit will have locating pins to help align parts, like the fuselage or wing halves of an aircraft. Most of the time these work fine and only occasionally do they cause a problem, which

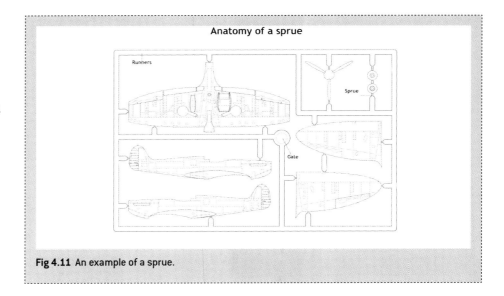

Anatomy of a sprue

Runners

Sprue

Gate

Fig 4.11 An example of a sprue.

we will come to later. On most kits you may spot small circular marks on parts, usually on the interior surfaces. These are caused by the ejector pins, small rods that push the formed plastic parts away from the mould.

Occasionally there may also be traces of an oily-looking substance on some plastic parts, this is the release agent, a lubricant that prevents the plastic sticking in the moulds. It can simply be removed using a small amount of water and washing-up liquid.

Another common problem that can occur on old kits – and sometimes even new ones – is flash. This is where molten plastic seeps in-between the two mould halves and cools, forming a web between parts, either because the pressure holding

the mould together is insufficient, or because the moulds are worn and no longer close up as tightly as before. Flash is usually so wafer thin that it can be easily removed using a sharp blade, either while the parts are still on the sprue, or as each part is removed and cleaned up.

Very rarely you might get short shots, where the plastic has failed to completely fill a cavity in the mould. In this instance it's almost impossible to repair or fix and the kit will either need to be returned or the manufacturer contacted for replacement parts.

SURFACE DETAIL

On almost all modern aircraft models the surface detail tends to be recessed or

Fig 4.12 An example of ejector pin marks, small circles on the plastic caused by the pins that help remove plastic from a mould.

Fig 4.13 An example of flash, caused by molten plastic seeping in between the two mould halves.

engraved; that is the panel line and any rivet detail is cut into the plastic. For many older aircraft kits the detail is raised; the panel lines and rivets stand proud of the surface. Recessed surface detail tends to be seen as more realistic, or at least less obtrusive than the raised kind, certainly when sanding down join lines where there is less risk of losing the detail. When it comes to painting and weathering, recessed panel lines also work well with washes, which we will cover in a later chapter. Ironically some modern kits reproduce what would be raised details on a full size subject (rivets, overlapping panels etc) with recessed details.

When it comes to raised detail, particularly on older kits where it may be excessively heavy, it can be toned down using wet and dry paper, or removed in its entirety and new panel lines engraved into the plastic using something as simple as a sewing needle in a drill chuck and a small steel rule as a guide, or with one of the specialist modelling tools like a P-Cutter and scribing templates. Some very old kits from the 1950s and 1960s, such as those from Aurora and Revell, used to have the positions of the markings and national insignia moulded to the plastic, which then required removal either by sanding away or filling. For the most part these kits rarely show up other than as second hand items at model shows or on eBay.

Surface detail is always a personal preference; in truth almost any kind of surface detail on an aircraft model from about 1:32 and smaller is going to be slightly over scale anyway, as what we usually see on a full size example viewed from a distance is the accumulation of dirt that collects in-between panels. But if kit companies stopped moulding surface detail in the interests of total accuracy, it would be conspicuous by its absence!

BEFORE YOU BEGIN

Carefully remove the sprues from the box, check them over and look for any missing, damaged or mis-moulded parts – it is important to do this now rather than later when you may be just about to add a crucial part to a near completed model only to find it is missing. A lot of kits include a sprue map included on the instruction sheet that helps as a guide.

If you do find anything missing or defective, either fill in the missing parts form (if there is one) or contact the retailer that sold you the kit. If possible check the kit before you buy it, though some kit packaging can make it hard to do this especially if sealed with tape, and shops can take a dim view on customers ripping open boxes – if in doubt, ask.

Study the instruction sheet carefully and familiarise yourself with the construction sequence. For the most part this is laid out in logical steps, but sometimes it may show items like undercarriage legs or tank tracks being added at an early stage when they would be better left off and added after the main assembly and painting stages have taken place. Once you are happy that the kit is complete, that you understand how it goes together and that you have all the tools you need, it is ready to start!

Perhaps the easiest method of removing parts from a sprue is to use side cutters though some smaller parts may be too delicate and this is where a modelling knife should be used, taking care not to damage the part concerned.

Depending on how neatly or closely you removed a part from the sprue, you may end up with a small piece of plastic attached to the kit part, and this is generally known as a sprue tag. The best way to deal with this is to carefully trim it away with a knife. Only remove the parts as needed for each assembly sequence.

TEST FIT EVERY PART.

Test fitting, or a dry run, is essential in making sure everything fits prior to applying paint or glue. Sometimes parts don't fit together because there is a slight mismatch or warpage. The kit may be an older example where the moulds have started to wear a little or, occasionally, it can be down to poor component design. In the case of an aircraft it is usually the fuselage and wings where a dry run is essential, on a tank it may be the joining of the hull to the chassis etc. Even

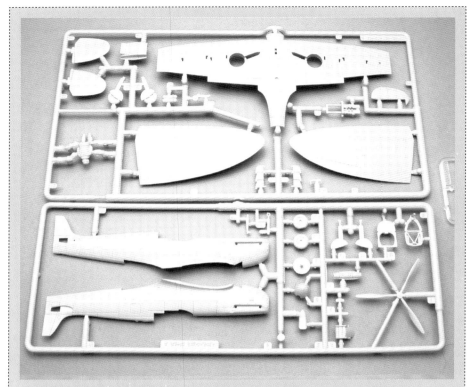

Fig 4.14 The sprues of the Airfix 1:72 Spitfire kit laid out. At this stage check that there is nothing missing or damaged.

the most experienced modellers sometimes forget to do this and only discover there is a problem with the glue already applied!

If problems do occur, take a step back and have a look at what may be causing the problem. Check each part thoroughly. There might be minute particles of plastic on the mating surfaces, either contamination in the mould or just wear and tear. A few swipes

with a sanding stick will usually solve the problem.

One of the most common reasons why some parts – say the two fuselage halves of an aeroplane – don't fit is that the locating pins may be out of alignment or the pin may be bigger than the hole. The simple fix is to remove the pin and gently give the mating surfaces a swipe of a sanding stick.

Fig 4.15 The safest way to remove parts from the sprue is to use a pair of side cutters.

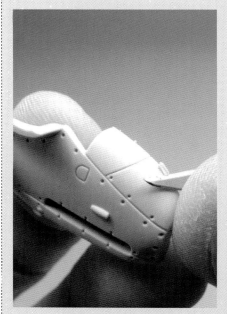

Fig 4.16 After removing from the sprue, any remaining tags or stubs of plastic can be carefully removed with a knife.

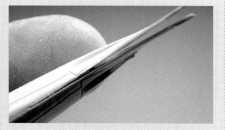

Fig 4.17 A dry run of this Spitfire fuselage shows the tail doesn't close up quite as tightly as intended.

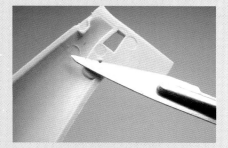

Fig 4.18 The problem is with one of the locating pins which is slightly too large. The solution is to either open up the corresponding hole with a file or remove the pin.

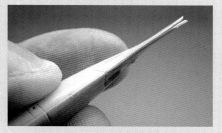

Fig 4.19 Problem solved and the two halves mate perfectly ready for gluing.

Persistent problems may be down to the age of the kit (the mould getting worn), parts shrinking slightly as they cool while in the mould, or just the design breakdown.

The key is not to rush things – problem solving is an important skill in modelling, every modeller old or new has to figure out some unexpected snag at some stage and learning how to deal with problems with one kit is invaluable experience that can be used on the next one.

PAINT AS YOU GO

Interior parts like aircraft cockpits, car interiors or the cabs of trucks should be painted during assembly because once parts are closed up it will be next to impossible to paint them. While advice in the past has been to paint as many parts on the sprue as possible, this isn't practical when you need to test fit some parts (like a cockpit interior), as there will always be seam lines to remove and liquid cement works better on a plastic-to-plastic contact meaning any paint will have to be scraped away. The same goes for plated parts which still need their mating surfaces cleaned up, even if using superglues, in order to get the strongest bond.

Some parts can be painted, like the details on a pilot figure, prior to cutting from a sprue, cleaning up and then painting the rest of the figure. Items like the insides of undercarriage doors are also best painted whilst in situ on the sprue.

Fig 4.20 The cockpit has been painted in Humbrol 78 (Cockpit Green) and the instrument panel decal applied.

Fig 4.21 Some parts are better painted on the sprue which can act as a convenient handle.

Fig 4.22 The tail planes are pushed into place and fixed using liquid cement applied with a brush.

Fig 4.23 The fuselage halves are held together and liquid cement is brushed on. Capillary action ensures the glue flows into the join.

STICKING POINT

When it comes to joining parts together, for example the fuselage of an aircraft, it is best to hold the parts loosely together and use a brush to apply liquid cement to the join. Capillary action means the glue will run into the join and you can then squeeze the parts together, wait a few moments (as the chemical weld begins) and then move onto the next section. If some plastic oozes up from the join, don't worry – this is normal,

just leave it to dry (overnight) and the plastic will have set hard and can be sanded down. Likewise if you happen to spill some liquid cement onto the surface, don't be tempted to mop it up as it will mar the plastic. Liquid cements evaporate so fast that the chances are it will have gone in a matter of minutes – all the more reason to use cement sparingly at all times.

Sometimes you may need to bind parts together while the glue sets; for example

there may be a minute amount of warpage or the parts flex too much – Airfix's 1:48 Buccaneer is a classic example where the fuselage parts flex considerably, but simple binding of the parts in sections using small tabs of tape soon solves this issue.

JOINS

Eliminating the seams or joins between glued parts is one of the key things that will separate a well made model from an

Fig 4.24 The basic wing parts of the Spitfire ready for assembly.

Fig 4.25 After removing the wings from the sprue, the mating surfaces are cleaned up using a sanding stick.

Fig 4.26 Liquid cement is applied to the wing root to help fix the wings onto the fuselage.

Fig 4.27 Strips of masking tape are used to bind the model together while the glue sets.

indifferently made one. It stops a model looking like an obvious collection of parts to replicating the look of the real thing.

Taking something like a fuselage and holding it up to a light source, you can see where the join falls because a very minute shadow is cast. This is where sanding comes in, to blend the two parts together. Working gently with a sanding stick or wet and dry paper, a few swipes will usually start to make the join disappear and progress can be checked by holding the part up to the light and seeing if the shadow has disappeared.

Usually if a join feels smooth to the touch it is generally dealt with, but a good method of checking seams on-the-fly is to brush a coat of matt paint (grey is a good neutral choice) along the join and allowing to dry – if the seam shows through then some further work is required and the process repeated, though in truth this only becomes laborious if dealing with kits that have ill-fitting parts. Some modellers like to use specialist products like Mr Surfacer, made in Japan, which is a hybrid primer/filler that plugs any minute gaps or cracks on a join, but any matt paint can be used for just checking seams.

If there are gaps remaining, or a slight step between parts that sanding alone won't fix, this is where filler comes into play. Rather than trying to apply filler straight to the model from the tube, it is best to squeeze a small blob onto a clean, dust-free surface (an old jar lid, plastic pot etc.) and then apply to the model using a toothpick or old paintbrush handle as a spatula. You have to work relatively fast as filler goes 'off' fairly quickly.

In some instances you can save filler, and protect adjacent surfaces on a model, by masking the join with tape. Let the filler dry for a few hours, preferably overnight, before sanding down. It has to be remembered that some fillers like Humbrol, Plasto and Squadron are solvent based, so applying too much can start to soften and weaken the plastic. If in doubt, it is better to apply filler in layers, allowing each to dry. If the amount of filler needed looks like being considerable — and this tends only to come into play for major conversion or reshaping work — then it may be better to use a water-based putty like Milliput.

NOSE WEIGHT

One problem that almost all aircraft modellers will at some stage face is in dealing with models with tricycle undercarriages — like airliners and modern jets — and the need to keep the model on all three legs. The problem is usually created by the model's centre of gravity being too far backward and so it ends up sitting on its tail, hence the phrase 'tail sitter'.

The most favoured and time honoured method of stopping a 'tail sitter' is to pack

Fig 4.28 Once the glue has set the resulting seam needs to be sanded down to improve the appearance of the model.

Fig 4.29 A sanding stick makes short work of this, starting with a coarse grit and finishing with a fine one.

Fig 4.30 The sanded join should be smooth to the touch and can be checked by holding the model up to a light source.

Fig 4.31 One way of protecting adjacement surface details when filling is to mask them with tape.

the model as far forward as possible with modelling clay or Blu-Tack mixed with small nuts and bolts, ball bearings or fisherman's weights. The further forward a model can be weighted, the less weight will be needed. For some subjects, like a glass-nosed B-26 with lots of interior details, only so much can be added up-front without it spoiling the look of the model. It is undesirable for the weights to be visible through the clear parts, so here the trick is to pack the engine nacelles as much as possible.

If your model is to be fixed to a baseboard or included as part of a diorama then it can simply be fixed into place using superglue or epoxy adhesive, though it does not hurt to drill some holes into the wheels to take a wire support to help keep the model firmly anchored. Sometimes it can be impossible, or least impractical, to add weight without putting so much into a model that the undercarriage collapses from the strain. Here it is time for a simple cheat to prop the model up – say a thin piece of wire or an oil drum under the rear fuselage or tail. Ironically the latter is not so improbable, as some real life aircraft often need propping up especially if undergoing maintenance or lacking sufficient fuel in the tanks to maintain the centre of gravity. Of course, making a model with landing up and fixing it to a display stand solves any worries about nose weighting!

Weighting isn't just needed for aircraft, however; many military modellers find that some form of weight in small scale armour models helps them sit on their tracks a little more realistically, especially if they are of the older vinyl 'rubber band' type. Likewise, weighting can be adding to the hulls of ship models, much like ballast in real life, only in this instance to keep them on their display stands.

SPARES BOX

One of the most valuable resources any modeller can build up is the 'spares box'. Most modern kits include alternative parts that may end up not being used, depending on which variant you have chosen to make. For example, the Airfix 1:72 Hurricane Mk.IIC kit has different parts to create either a Sea Hurricane or a 'tropical' version, which is fitted with a Vokes filter in a large chin fairing under the cowling. Whatever parts you don't use go into the spares box.

The simplest method of starting off a spares box is to use an old kit box for storage. As your collection of parts start to grow you may wish to start sorting them into different categories, say one box for aircraft parts, another for tanks, ships etc. Experienced modellers, with a collection of spare parts built up over the years, are more thorough and sort their collection out into bombs, drop tanks or missiles. DIY storage boxes, with separate plastic trays or compartments, can be had very cheaply and are ideal for storing and sorting your collection of spare parts.

Fig 4.32 Basic tool boxes like these can be found in bargain stores and are ideal for organising your spares. This one contains various aircraft stores and parts collected over several years of modelling.

Fig 4.33 A damaged clear part from a kit, in this case a Sea Harrier canopy that has been scuffed in transit.

Even failed modelling projects can be salvaged for spares and the rest of the model used as a test-bed for paints.

CLEAR PARTS

Perhaps the most delicate parts in any kit are the transparent or clear parts as they are very unforgiving if damaged or if any mistakes are made in preparation and final fitting to the model.

In some very rare situations you may need to sand clear parts, either to reshape or repair them or because they have a mould-line down the middle of a canopy – this is because the part is moulded in two halves to get the correct cross-section and to facilitate removal from the mould.

Clear parts can be sanded and polished back to new, but it does require the right tools and techniques, not to mention confidence, to get the best results. To remove a blemish or mould-line from a clear part start by using a very fine grit sanding stick, wet and dry paper or nail buffing pad, preferably with a drop of water with washing-up liquid added. The plastic will go matt and opaque, but clarity begins to be restored by polishing with finer grits. It is often best to keep the sanding strokes in the same direction and to work slowly and methodically.

Ultra fine sanding sticks will begin to polish the plastic (it will feel warm to the touch) and for a finishing touch there are specific plastic polishes available though something as simple as toothpaste or the polishing creams that come with CD and DVD cleaning sets can be used as a rubbing compound to buff the parts up to a shine.

Dab a bit on using a soft cloth and gently work into the plastic until it has started to disappear, then using a clean cloth (an old piece of denim is ideal for this) continue polishing the plastic and it should look new again. Try to avoid metal polishes as some contain chemicals (like ammonia) that can weaken and craze plastic very quickly, ruining parts.

Some modellers like to seal this shine by dipping clear parts in an acrylic floor polish like Future or Pledge, wicing away the excess and allowing to dry. Alternatively a coat of gloss varnish can impart a high shine should you require it, though be aware that oil-based varnishes can yellow over time so an acrylic varnish may be a better choice.

FRAMING

Painting the framing on an aircraft canopy can sometimes tax a beginner, especially if it is attempted freehand – then inexperienced modellers wonder why the paint dries translucent or the frame lines are not as neat as they would have liked.

Perhaps the oldest trick in the book is not to paint the frame lines at all, but to simulate them using tape. Take a piece of (clean) Sellotape or Magic Tape, and smooth it down over a dust-free surface, either a

Fig 4.34 Using a fine sanding stick, the damaged plastic is carefully sanded down.

Fig 4.35 Finer grades of sanding sticks are used to progressively smooth out the scratches.

Fig 4.36 Plastic polish and soft cloth restore the chine and clarity.

Fig 4.37 With all the major assembly done and all joins rubbed down, the model is ready for priming and painting.

cutting mat or a scrap of wood. If, for example, you are making a Hurricane and it requires the canopy to be painted Dark Earth, then paint the tape this colour and allow it dry thoroughly. Using a ruler (a steel rule is preferable) carefully cut lines to the required width and then apply to your canopy. Trim away any excess tape and you should have a canopy that looks neater than trying to hand paint it.

Experienced modellers utilise a similar technique, though they use commercially available clear decal film and will start by painting the interior colour of the frame (i.e. grey/green on a Hurricane), allowing it to dry, then applying the camouflage colour and cutting and applying the frame just as they would any water-slide decal. The trick with the grey/green is that when viewed from certain angles it looks as though the interior of the framing has been painted with the cockpit colour as per the original machine.

Other methods for painting canopies involve masking them with tape or liquid masks, but we'll cover these in the next chapter, which deals specifically with painting.

PRACTISE!

There is no substitute for experience and that only comes with practise. The one thing to stress about modelling is that mistakes will happen and that you can sometimes learn more from what you do wrong than what you did right. It is a natural part of the learning process; every modeller who has ever made a kit has fouled something up at some stage — some after decades of making models! So, as disappointing as it is, you can always use it to your advantage.

If a project doesn't go quite right don't be tempted to throw it away. Either strip it down for bits that can be saved for the spares box or use the model as a test-bed to try out paints, finishes and techniques — you can learn so much about painting (either by brush, airbrush or spray can) by practising on a 'junk' model.

Step by step build 1 by Brian Canell

1:72 North American F-86F Sabre

1:72 AIRFIX NORTH AMERICAN F-86F SABRE

Airfix's 1:72 F-86F Sabre is an ideal starter project for anyone looking to add a jet fighter to their collection. The Sabre was one of the first truly great jet fighters and made its name over the skies of Korea in the 1950s. **see Fig 1.1.**

Airfix have also modelled the radar-equipped F-86D 'Sabredog' variant, which was first released in 1975 and was last available in the late 1980s – it is now a collector's item! The 2010 Sabre kit depicts the '6/3' hard-wing version of the F-86. Two boxings are available – one with USAF and Italian markings (A03082), the other with RAF and Yugoslavian markings (A03083).

This particular Sabre forms part of the 2011 Airfix Club Kit (which also includes the Sabre's adversary, the MiG 15) and provides decals for 'Little Rita', flown by Lt. Dick Geiger of the 16th Fighter Interceptor Squadron, 51st Fighter Wing based at Suwon Airbase, South Korea between 1952 and 1953. **see Fig 1.2.** However, the plastic parts are the same in all the kits.

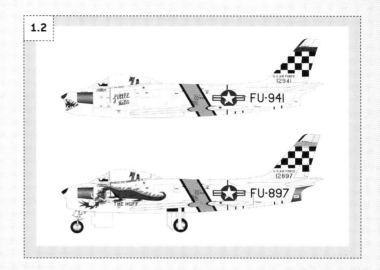

1.2

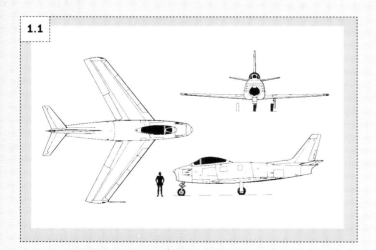

1.1

COCKPIT

There are five main parts to build the cockpit: the seat, control column, tub, armoured bulkhead and instrument panel, all of which are painted grey H140 with red H153 seat cushion and headrest. The control column is aluminium H53 with a matt black grip. There are three decals to apply for instrument panels and side consoles, but apply the instrument panel decal prior to fitting the kit part so the bottom corners tuck behind the front edges of the tub. **see Figs 1.3 and 1.4.**

The kit includes a pilot figure, which adds a touch of scale to the model. His flight jacket is painted Olive Drab H66, his flight suit trousers are US Light Green H117 and his life jacket is lemon H99, finished with black boots and gloves, and a white helmet **see Fig 1.5.**

As with most model aircraft with a tricycle undercarriage, some nose weight will be needed to stop the tail dropping. Here Airfix have provided a handy little box section in which you can add some weight. Also moulded into the upper air intake is the amount of

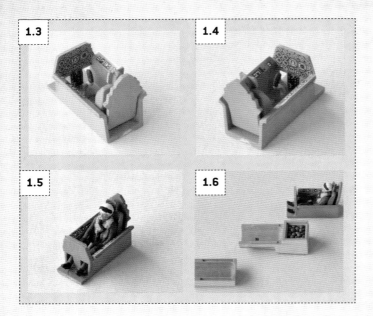

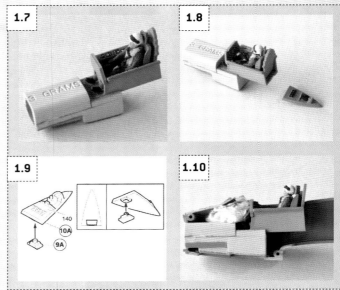

weight you need (3 grams). Lead shot was used to fill the box – its 'lid' will be the cockpit floor **see Figs 1.6 and 1.7**. The next two parts to glue together are the rear cockpit interior under the rear canopy and a retaining piece **see Figs 1.8 and 1.9**. Unusually for a 1:72 scale model this canopy can be made to operate.

With the cockpit completed, the front wheel well and air intake can be added to one fuselage side. Some extra nose weight was added using lead shot wrapped in cling film and wedged behind the instrument panel **see Fig 1.10**.

Prior to joining the fuselage halves together you need to install the tailpipe and locate the upper rear cockpit part into its slot without cement so it can slide. Then cement the fuselage halves. The fit is nice and tight but you may need a few dots of filler where the parts were cut from the sprue **see Fig 1.11**.

The wings are moulded in three parts; one lower piece and two upper pieces. There are choices for either drop tanks or bombs – if you want to include either you'll need to open up two pairs of holes

on the inside of the lower wing. The rear stabilizers were glued in place but note that, unlike many aircraft, they are not at right angles to the fuselage – the correct dihedral is 80° **see Fig 1.12**.

To make painting easier, the main undercarriage legs can be fitted into place so that the model can stand upright while the paint is drying. The main undercarriage legs can be added too **see Fig 1.13**. Here the instructions suggest you glue them in the open position with the undercarriage lowered but references suggest that the doors are closed at all times unless the undercarriage was actually being operated. Note that fuel drop tanks have not yet been added as there are decals to apply first.

Another option in the kit is either open or closed air brakes and access panels on the fuselage forward of the wing root.

The last parts to add before painting was the canopy assembly. Using either Humbrol Clearfix or PVA glue (as mentioned in previous chapters) cement the front canopy first and then very carefully add a line of glue on the edge of the sliding rear cockpit **see Fig 1.14**.

1.11

1.12

80° 80°

1.13

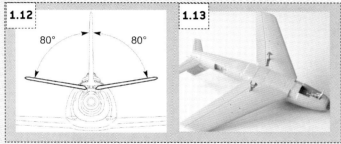

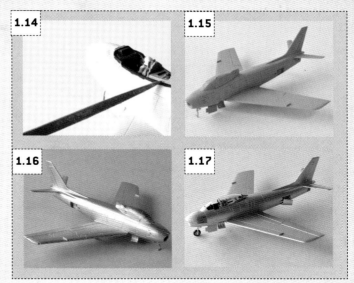

1.14

1.15

1.16

1.17

PAINTING

Tamiya tape was used to mask the canopy; this is preferred by many modellers as it follows the contours on a model very well and does not leave any residue when it is peeled off. The aircraft was then primed with Humbrol H1 Primer acrylic aerosol and this was left to cure for a day or two **see Fig 1.15**.

Most Sabres of the Korean War period were unpainted aluminium or a Natural Metal Finish (NMF). There are a number of different ways this can be replicated: a can of automotive silver paint (available from Halfords in the UK), a variety of paints to create a variation on metal tone, speciality 'metalizer' paints (like SNJ, Alclad2 or Gunze) that can be buffed (sometimes in conjunction with metal

polishing powders), or thin metal foils. A simple but effective natural metal finish can be created using Humbrol's Metalcote H27002 Polished Aluminium. Although this can be brushed on, it is better applied with an airbrush. Metalcote tends to be less grainy than usual silver paint and it can be lightly polished with a soft cloth to make it more effective, especially if you mask off different panels and vary the amount of polishing. Three light coats were applied and, although it is touch dry in minutes, the paint is best left to cure thoroughly for a few days **see Fig 1.16**.

The masking tape was removed and a couple of coats of Johnson's Klear floor polish were applied to seal the finish as metallic paints can rub off with too much handling. Because Klear is water based it doesn't craze or lift the oil-based Metalcote. The insides of the air brakes and access panels were painted with Interior Green H226 with silver detailing. Finally the gun port panels and the area around the tailpipe were brushed with Gunmetal H53 and the airbrake doors and actuators were installed **see Fig 1.17**.

DECALS AND FINISHING

The original Airfix Sabre kit from over thirty years ago only had decals for the main markings, mainly 'Stars and Bars' and squadron colours – conversely, the new Airfix Sabre has nearly 90 decals, most of which are maintenance stencils, instructions and warnings.

Because of the sheer number of stencils it is best to apply the main markings first, especially the band around the fuselage which will have a number of stencils added on top later on. The fuselage 'Stars and Bars' are in two pieces so there is no need to cut them if you want to display your aircraft with the airbrakes open.

There are two decals for the fuselage band, apply the small one first to the centre of the fuselage underside and then add the larger upper one lining up the forward point to the rear of the canopy. When it comes to adding large numbers of decals like this there is no substitute for patience, but the end result is well worth it **see Figs 1.18 and 1.19.**

With the decals applied, the final touches can be installed, such as the aerial on the underside of the rear fuselage and the pitot tube in the right wing. The drop tanks can also now be added. The whole model can then be sealed using another coat of Klear and any weathering applied – on this model it was decided to keep it clean, as befits a well-maintained aircraft where every ounce of speed was needed in combat **see Fig 1.20.**

As a companion piece or future project, what better than the Sabre's adversary, the MiG15? This is the North Korean scheme from the 2011 Airfix Club Members set, providing an interesting contrast not only in colour schemes and markings, but in the context of early jet fighter development **see Figs 1.21-1.23.**

1.18

1.19

1.20

1.21

1.22

1.23

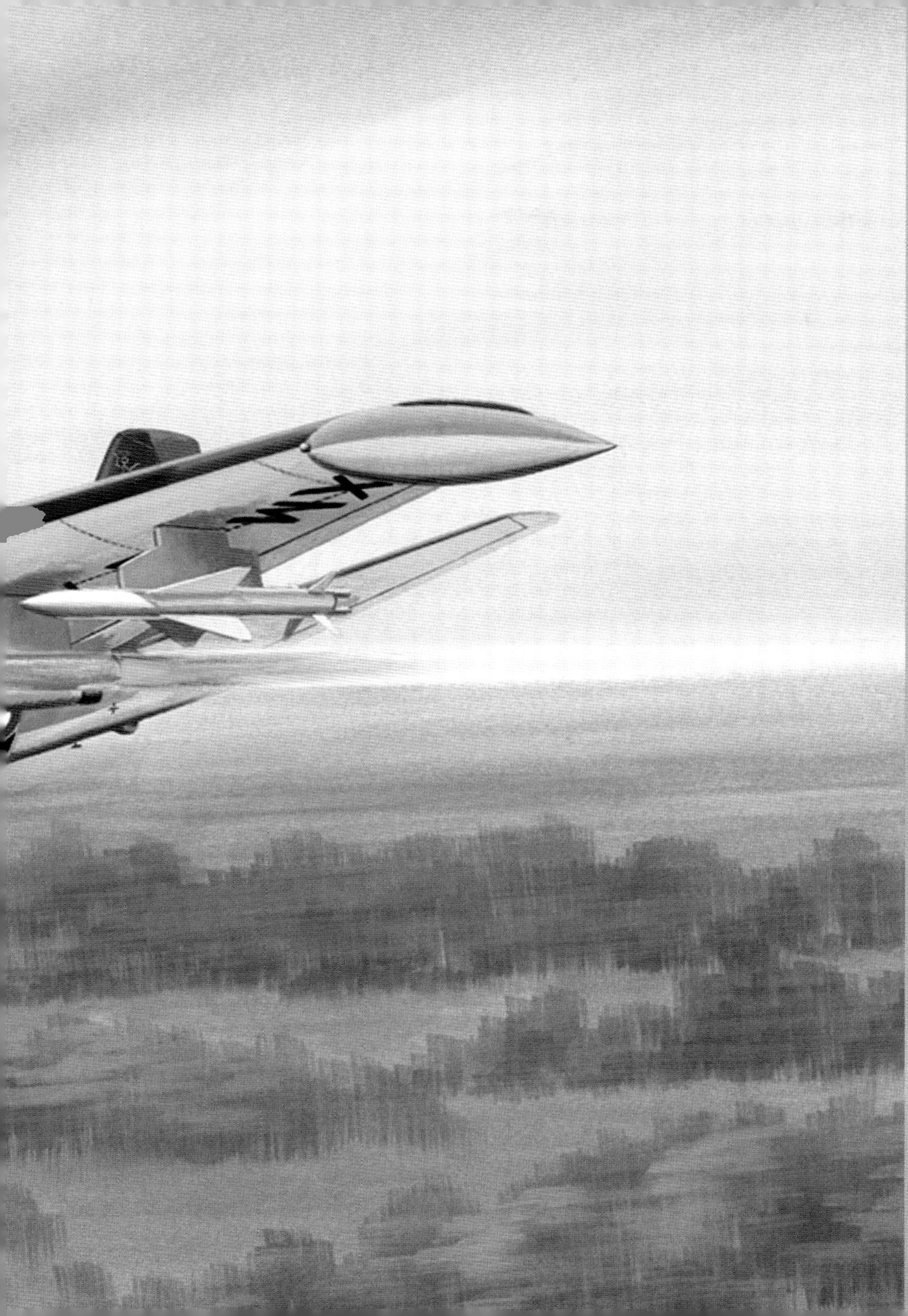

CHAPTER 5 Painting

PAINTING

Most modellers will admit that when they first started making model kits, paint rarely came into it and decals would end up being applied to unpainted plastic. Some model companies tended to mould their kits in approximate colours – red for a Red Arrows Hawk, or silver for a P-47D Thunderbolt – perhaps subconsciously aware that a large portion of their market, probably younger modellers, never touched a paintbrush. It was Matchbox in the 1970s who chose to capitalise on this by making their kits in 'colour', moulding whole sprues in different colours that, while never able to capture complex camouflage patterns, occasionally approximated the actual colours – red and white for an Alpha Jet – and sometimes not – pink and blue for a P-51D Mustang!

In the 1950s and 60s the novice modeller had very few options when it came to painting – in the UK, for example, modellers were basically limited to a few paints from the likes of Airfix and Humbrol. These were enamels that came in bottles or tinlets, usually gloss and not matched to any colour standards to allow a truly accurate finish to be obtained. More experienced modellers took to mixing their paints to achieve the desired colours, but the only way to make a paint matt was usually to add talcum powder to the paint before use.

By the 1960s a larger variety of paints began to arrive on the market, predominately enamels, but now available in matt straight from the tin, and often with better matches to real world colours – painting a Spitfire or Messerschmitt became much easier. In the early 70s the Humbrol 'Authentic' range arrived. These were paints accurately matched to the references of the day and covered subjects including WWII RAF, Luftwaffe, US Navy, Axis aircraft, through to military colours and modern air forces. Modellers could now buy paint straight from the rack for their chosen subjects and be assured that the colours were correct – the only caveat being that the colours were accurate by the research standards of the day! The Authentic line remained an integral part of the Humbrol catalogue until 1986, when the entire range was dropped, with Humbrol instead choosing to greatly expand their basic range of paints, though many of the former Authentic colours did migrate into the standard range.

It was against this backdrop in the eighties that the paint market underwent a revolution. Many new paint ranges came on the scene, all proclaiming their accuracy and ease of use to the modeller. Gloy released a large range in the early eighties, as did Precision, but one of the biggest revolutions came in 1984 with a company called Compucolor. They claimed their paints were matched to original samples by computer for a truly accurate, repeatable colour match. Compucolor only lasted a couple of years before the company split into two, with one half becoming Compucolor 2 and the other DBI paints. Of these companies, only Precision remains in business today, catering largely to the model railway market.

The mid 1980s also saw the introduction of a range of paints by the UK mail order company Hannants called Xtracolor. Ironically these returned to the roots of the original enamel paints by being gloss in nature – over the decades modellers realised that decals take better to a gloss finish than matt – but offered a huge range of accurately matched colours that remain available to this day and are a popular choice for the more advanced enthusiast.

For most modellers who are new to the hobby and looking for their first experience with using modelling paints, Humbrol remain the most popular choice, especially when it comes to hand painting. There is a wide range, they are readily available and the Airfix painting instructions are matched to Humbrol paint numbers, removing the guesswork of colour matching for the modeller.

THE ACRYLIC REVOLUTION

In Japan, Tamiya and Gunze Sanyo also had their own rapidly expanding line of paints, but unlike their western counterparts, the Japanese preferred to develop water-based acrylics rather than oil-based enamels. Also noteworthy is the Mr Color range of acrylic lacquers, a more specialised paint that can produce stunning results when airbrushed.

While acrylics did encounter some initial resistance from Western modellers who were more used to traditional enamels, this changed when they became aware of the often superior spraying properties of acrylics.

By the end of the 1980s, Humbrol also began to develop a line of acrylics based around the most popular colours in their enamel range, and these continue to be expanded. Revell also invested in acrylics with their 'Aqua' range, as well increasing their own line of enamels. Hannants subsequently added an acrylic equivalent to their range – Xtracrylix – to compliment their Xtracolor line.

One of the more interesting acrylic paint developments in recent years is the Vallejo line from Spain which offers three ranges; Vallejo Air, a pre-thinned paint ready for airbrushing; Model Colour, a more general range suitable for hand brushing; and Panzer Aces, for military modellers.

Perhaps the biggest advantage acrylics have over enamels is that they are often low odour, non-toxic and easily cleaned with water. They have gained popularity hugely in the last few years, with modellers both new and veteran switching to them. About the only disadvantages with acrylics are that, in inexperienced hands, they can be tricky to hand brush, starting to dry within seconds of being applied to a model, and attempts to smooth the rapidly drying paint can pull up underlying coats and result in a very rough finish and a dispirited modeller. Though enamels take longer to dry, they are easier to work with when hand painting and will often give a smoother, superior finish – the flip side is that the fast drying time of acrylics actually works better when it comes to spraying. There are tricks and methods that can be used to retard acrylics for hand brushing, and we'll touch on these shortly.

BRUSHES

It's very rare that new or inexperienced modellers start out painting their first few models with an airbrush and by far the vast majority will begin with the humble paintbrush. These can vary vastly in quality, from very cheap synthetic brushes costing literally pence, to artist's quality sable brushes that can cost many pounds. It is

Fig 5.1 Today's modeller has a wide range of paints to choose from, both enamel and acrylic.

often said that modellers should buy the best paintbrushes they can afford and with good reason – it is true.

Cheap paint brushes do modellers no favours; they are often coarse, do not hold their shape, offer little control and, more unfortunately, often shed hairs onto the wet paintwork. Buying brushes can often be an afterthought, especially with younger modellers where they are either expected to use those that come with starter or gift sets, or are bought a set on the basis of cost rather than quality. And while the cost of brushes has stabilised, if not come down, over the years, it is still worth investing in the best quality, which means spending a little more, perhaps the cost of two or three entry-level kits to get a good selection of brushes.

The best places to go shopping for quality paint brushes are art shops that specialise in brands like Windsor and Newton, Daler-Rowney, etc. and are likely to have a good selection of quality materials. Sable brushes remain the first choice as the bristles tend to be very soft and help eliminate brush strokes. Advances in synthetic bristles over the years have yielded brushes that can be as good as traditional sable hairs, sometimes at a more competitive price. In buying a brush, look at the bristles and see if they are a good shape. Any brush that looks splayed or has hairs sticking out at angles should be avoided. If possible, stroke the brush across the palm of your hand – if the brush remains firm but the feel is silky, chances are it is of good quality. Too firm, or the brush feels scratchy to the touch, then it is probably too harsh for model painting. If in doubt, ask – most art stores will be only too happy to assist with advice if you explain what you need.

For painting small details a 000 or 00 is best. This brush has a small, finely pointed tip that can hold and control small quantities of paint with precision. Next are some medium rounds from a 1 through to 3 which are better for painting medium sized areas, like the uniforms on figures, cockpit interiors etc. For painting larger surfaces, like aircraft, tanks or ships, you will need a couple of flat brushes.

Sometimes bargains can be had and if you see a competitively priced brush that you like the look of, it is worth giving it a try

– at the very worst the brush can be used for secondary painting duties.

If you've spent good money on your brushes then it is essential to look after that investment by taking care of them. As much as it's a cliché that good brushes can last a lifetime, this is true and many experienced modellers will have brushes going back 10, 20 or even 30 years that are as good as the day they were bought because they have been carefully and properly looked after.

As soon as any painting has finished, gently squeeze any excess paint out of the bristles using a piece of tissue or rag. Do this a couple of times until the brush appears clean. For washing brushes have a jar of cleaner nearby, either white spirit if using enamels or water (with a dash of detergent) for acrylics. Dip the brush in and swirl it around a few times; the cleaner may start to become cloudy as residue in the brush is dissolved and dislodged. Take the brush out and carefully squeegee onto your clean piece of rag. Repeat this process several times; if the rag remains clean as you squeeze the bristles through it then the brush is free of paint. Experienced modellers like to keep two jars of cleaner handy, using the second as a final rinse to make sure the brush is thoroughly cleaned. Additionally a final rinse in a clean jar of water/detergent, whether using enamels or acrylics, helps condition the bristles. There are some commercial brush conditioners available and some modellers even use hair

Fig5.2 Half a dozen quality paintbrushes, from a 000 to a 1/4 inch flat, are a good investment.

Fig 5.3 Excess paint is removed from the brush prior to cleaning and rinsing in thinner.

Fig 5.4 After being rinsed in a jar of thinner and wiped again, the process is repeated until the brush is clean.

conditioner as it works on the same principles for a paintbrush.

With the brush cleaned it should be stored carefully, preferably upright and any protective cap replaced. One trick to help keep a point on fine brush is to draw it through your lips, but it goes without saying that should only be done once the brush has been thoroughly cleaned and dried. Try to avoid the temptation to soak a brush by leaving it standing on its bristles in jar – this is a sure-fire way to damaging the brush and ruining the shape.

If a brush has been accidentally allowed to dry out it can be resurrected using commercial DIY brush cleaners, but special care has to be taken in using these as they often contain quite aggressive chemicals. Once the bristles have softened sufficiently, repeat the cleaning process previously described. Bear in mind that there are only a few times that even a quality paint brush can survive such a deep post-cleaning process, so it is best to avoid it by taking care of them from the outset.

If you do damage a brush to the point that it is no longer usable for quality painting, don't throw it out just yet, it may prove valuable for less-kindly jobs that might damage a quality brush, like drybrushing and applying pastels and pigments – the same goes for cheaper brushes.

PREPARATION

Once a model is assembled and seam lines, gaps and the like have been dealt with, give the model a good dusting with a stiff brush or an old toothbrush to dislodge any dust that may have accumulated in panel lines or recessed corners from sanding and cleaning up join lines. Check it over one more time for any construction defects and amend where necessary. Some modellers like to give a their model a quick clean with the kinds of alcohol-based wipes used for cleaning computer screens or CDs – these will pick up any remaining mould release agent or skin grease and leave the surface clean and ready for painting.

Many modellers like to apply primer or an undercoat before applying the final paint finish. The advantage of a primer is that it will show up any remaining flaws in the assembly work, and allow the modeller to go back and rework them. Primers are also essential if trying to paint light colours over dark plastic as they provide a neutral base tone to work with. Primer coats can be of almost any paint the modeller chooses, but usually a light grey colour is best – Humbrol 64 light grey is ideal. More advanced modellers may like to use automotive aerosol paints and we'll come to them later.

Before applying a coat of primer, it is essential to ensure the paint is thoroughly mixed – this also applies to the subsequent colour coats. Enamels, in particular, tend to separate out into a heavy pigment at the

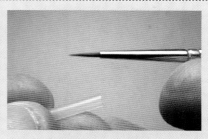

Fig 5.5 Round brushes should be shaped to a point before being returned to their protective cap.

Fig 5.6 This brush has seen better days, but can still be used for drybrushing and weathering.

Fig 5.7 An old toothbrush can be used to clean panel lines and remove dust prior to giving the model a coat of primer.

Fig 5.8 After shaking the tin, give it a good stir and shake again until all the pigment is dispersed.

Fig 5.9 After use, give the rim a wipe clean to avoid paint deposits building up.

Fig 5.10 If not you could end up with a tin like this!

bottom of the tin with a lighter, oily carrier liquid floating on top. This needs to be thoroughly mixed together before use and this can be easily done using a suitable stirring stick – a screwdriver, a coffee stirrer, even a length of sprue or the end of a paintbrush will do the job. Make sure you stir thoroughly and get all of the pigment from the bottom corners of the pot mixed in. Replace the lid tightly and give the tin a good shake. This may take five minutes or more of constant stirring and shaking, but is essential to the final job. One trick is to add a couple of ball-bearings to act as agitators in the paint – the more you can hear them rattling around inside the tin, the more the paint is starting to mix properly. Once done the tin should contain a thickish, creamy liquid of one colour with no streaks, lumps or separate oil in it.

Take a small amount of paint onto your chosen brush (for something like the underside of the Spitfire use a medium sized flat brush) and wipe any excess off on the side of the tin. Use broad, long strokes on your model to lay paint onto the surface, working it into any recessed detail as you go. When a section has been covered begin to work back over the paint in one direction – such as the front to back with the airflow on the real thing. This will smooth the paint down into a nice, even coat. Work on sections of the model at a time. As mentioned, the beauty of enamels is in the drying time – it will remain wet enough to blend sections together. If you do start to feel the paint 'drag' at any point or encounter any resistance you can very slightly wet your brush with white spirit to smooth the paint back down. Depending on the colour of the plastic, it may take a couple of coats to prime the model – always allow plenty of time for each coat to dry.

Once you have finished with your tin of paint, give the rim a quick wipe to remove any excess paint that may have collected there.

THE COLOUR AND THE SHAPE

When painting a model, there are a couple of general rules that apply. Dark colours will cover lighter colours better than light colours cover dark, so working from the lightest colours through to the darkest is invariably the best route — as mentioned, this is where a primer coat helps, especially if painting light colours on dark plastic.

In looking at a model such a Spitfire Mk.I, this will involve painting the underside first. In this instance, a coat of Humbrol 90 to represent the 'Sky' shade used, before moving on to the darker upper surface camouflage of Dark Green and Dark Earth. At this stage there is no need to worry about the demarcation between upper and lower colours, simply paint the Sky colour some distance past where the actual demarcation is in real life. Using these techniques you will find that it takes no more than a few minutes to cover the underside of a small model.

Again, do not attempt to get complete coverage in one coat, it's very unlikely you will manage this and obtain a smooth thin coat. In fact, the biggest mistake beginners and less experienced modellers make is to try and cover a model all in one go. It is perfectly normal to have to apply more than one coat to achieve total coverage, and multiple thin coats are always preferable to one thick one. Allow the paint plenty of drying time (six hours is normal for enamels, but overnight is preferable). Painting is one stage of modelling where patience will pay dividends with the final result. Between coats you can always check for any rough spots or hairs in your finish, and can remove them either with the tip of a blade or a needle or by very lightly sanding the affected area.

Once satisfied with the underside colour, it is time to move on to the topside and the camouflage. Aircraft such as the Spitfire Mk.I had a hard edged demarcation between the upper and lower surface colours. Beginners are often tempted to attempt such a division line freehand just painting along the division line whilst trying to keep their hand steady - this will never really result in a straight, sharp line. The best way to achieve this is to mask the division line out. Many years ago pretty much the only masking material available was Sellotape, a clear plastic tape that will yield a very sharp line, but it is also inflexible and has a very harsh adhesive that can rip paint up when removed. These days there are better, more flexible masking tapes available cheaply from any DIY or automotive store, as well as numerous kinds of masking tape specially aimed at the modelling fraternity. These are thinner than traditional masking tape and tend to be very flexible for making curves whilst having a low tack adhesive which prevents underlying paint being torn up. The only downside is that these tapes are relatively expensive but they are worth the investment.

In order to get the best results from masking, a couple of tools will be very useful – a flat, hard cutting surface (a piece of glass or a bathroom tile) or a clean cutting mat; a fresh, sharp blade and a straight edge such as a steel rule. Many

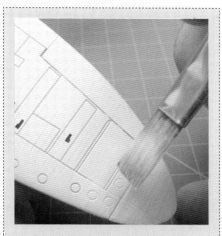

Fig 5.11 Undersides being painted.

people will use masking tape straight from the roll, but this can cause problems — the edge of a roll of masking tape is subject to damage, which can affect the masked edge. It's far better to use freshly cut tape that has a sharp edge with no damage. Lay out a piece of tape and cut it into strips which can then be used to mark the division line between upper and lower colours. If you have painted the underside colour high enough there will be a line of paint above your masked line in the area of the upper surface camouflage. You need only mask a thin line, as unless you are particularly clumsy when applying the following colours, your brush should not go over the masking tape into the underside area.

With the lower colour masked off, work can now begin on the upper surface colours.

Humbrol 29 Dark Earth is applied using the same techniques for the underside colour and it may take two coats in order to obtain a smooth, even finish. Take care to brush away from the masked lines and not toward them in order to minimise any paint build up along the masked edge.

With the Dark Earth areas thoroughly dry, it is time to apply the Dark Green camouflage. With very few exceptions, camouflage patterns – particularly on something like a Spitfire – were not random but were laid down in official documents and drawings to be followed when painting the real aircraft.

An old trick is to mark out the camouflage pattern using a soft pencil, but this can just as easily be achieved with the camouflage colour itself. Use a medium sized brush (it can be either flat or round depending on your preference) and, with a little paint, begin outlining a section one at a time before filling the pattern in, constantly referring to the finishing instructions as you go. Although enamels have a long drying time, if you mark the entire camouflage pattern out first, the outlines may have already started to dry by the time you come fill the colour in, and this can result in an uneven finish. Instead work slowly and methodically, one section at a time until the entire pattern is filled in.

Fig 5.12 There are several methods of masking, from liquids to low-tack tape.

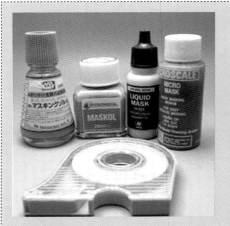

Fig 5.13 A thin strip of tape is used to mark out the demarcation between the upper and lower camouflage colours, before the rest of the undersides are masked off.

Fig 5.14 Dark earth being applied.

Fig 5.15 Working a section at a time, the outline of the camouflage is marked out with dark green before filling in.

CANOPIES

One of the trickiest things any budding modeller can face at the painting stage is painting the frame lines on canopies and clear parts. Most attempt to paint them freehand and the results are frames that look messy where the paint has strayed onto the 'glass' areas where it shouldn't. The trick is to use the finest brush to hand and apply small quantities of paint at a time. It may take several coats to build up a truly opaque finish and if any paint strays onto the clear areas, this can be removed when dry using a toothpick or a section of sprue shaped to a point, taking care not to scratch the plastic.

There are several approaches to painting frame lines, and they often depend on how well moulded (or not) the frame detail is in a kit. As mentioned previously perhaps the easiest method is the old trick of taking a strip of Sellotape, painting it the appropriate colours and then cutting into thin strips. This can work on some subjects where straight lines are needed, but falls down where the inflexibility of the tape won't follow complex, curved surfaces.

A variation on this is to paint clear decal film (available from many online model retailers), cut into strips then soak and apply as a normal decal. This offers more finesse and control, but again can be tricky when it comes to curved shapes. Perhaps the most foolproof, albeit more labour intensive, method is to mask out the frame lines. When it comes to spray painting

this is essential. Where the frame lines are heavy and well marked, this can sometimes be done using a liquid masking agent like Maskol, by carefully applying the solution to the clear areas with a toothpick, making sure it butts-up to the edges of the frame.

On some kits this may not be practical, so marking out the edges of the framing with thin strips of tape comes into play, and this technique certainly does allow more flexibility (literally) in being able to follow and mask tricky curved surfaces. The remaining areas can then either be filled with a liquid mask or more sections of tape.

There are commercially available ready-made masks designed for specific kits and these can certainly take the guesswork and labour out of masking, albeit at a price.

One trick worth remembering is to give the frames a coat of the equivalent cockpit interior colour before adding the subsequent colour coats. Once the canopy is complete this can create the impression of the interior of the frames being painted, as per actual aircraft.

SPRAY PAINTING

There used to be a time when airbrushes were very much the reserve of the well heeled modeller, not only because of the cost of the airbrush itself, but also because of the expense of the compressor needed to provide power. These days airbrush equipment, while still a financial

Fig 5.16 With the basic camouflage colours applied, the model is ready for a coat of gloss varnish and decals.

Fig 5.17 Masking clear parts is essential when spray painting. This Spitfire canopy has been protected using masking tape on the straight sections and Maskol on the curved surfaces of the windscreen.

commitment, is more accessible than ever before.

In terms of developing modelling skills, airbrushing takes some time to master – in fact even experienced users will say they learn something new all the time – but the benefits of airbrushing over brush painting are many. Generally a sprayed coat will cover better than a brushed coat, whilst at the same time being much thinner, preserving detail that can so easily be lost when applying multiple coats of paint with a brush.

One route to gaining experience in spray painting is to use aerosol cans and many manufacturers now produce their own spray paints in a wide range of colours for modellers. Some modellers, while preferring to hand paint their models, will use spray varnishes for a final coat as this can provide a uniformity of finish not easily achieved with a brush, especially as it can help conceal brush marks. The down side to spray cans is a lack of control, with no way to regulate the spray pattern, and a tendency for some to lay down an overly thick coat of paint, although with advances in paint and materials technology this is not as much of an issue as it once was. When it comes to single colour finishes, like white, silver or even black, spray cans often produce a finish superior to brush painting. Certainly when it comes to modelling cars, spray cans come into their own, especially with ranges of automotive paint that can be used on their small-scale counterparts.

Fig 5.18 This cockpit opening has been protected with soft facial tissues topped with a coat of Maskol to seal the edges.

Fig 5.19 Aerosol cans of grey primer offer a fast way of undercoating a model and the chance to gain experience using spray paints.

The key to using spray cans is to shake them vigorously so that the agitator inside rattles around mixing the paint, solvent and propellant together. Begin by spraying ahead of the model and continue past before stopping – if you start and stop on the model, you may end up with spatters from paint that has collected on the nozzle. Always work in light coats – some spray paints dry very fast, so you can reapply another coat sometimes in a matter of 10 or 15 minutes. Always observe safety precautions when using spray cans. After use, invert the can and continue spraying until no paint comes out of the nozzle.

With care and clever masking techniques even spray cans can produce an award winning finish, and these days they can form an important part of any modeller's arsenal, even with experienced airbrush users.

AIRBRUSHES

But as good and useful as spray cans are, there are some things that the airbrush excels at, especially when it comes to soft edged camouflage patterns, or the kinds of mottle finishes seen on Luftwaffe aircraft and German WW2 military vehicles. To this end it is the effect of seeing other people's models finished using airbrushes that leads inevitably to a desire to use and own them.

There are a host of manufacturers and styles of airbrush available to the modeller,

Fig 5.20 The best finish is obtained by spraying with primer, using light, even coats.

Fig 5.21 The Badger 200, a siphon-fed, single-action airbrush that has been a popular choice with modellers for generations.

from the most basic of spray guns to high end, professional artist's equipment. A general rule is to buy the very best that you can afford. A cheap spray gun will provide a very nice finish, but its limitations will be exposed very quickly when the enthusiastic modeller wishes to try new techniques, so it's worth the extra cost (which needn't be excessive) to go for the best airbrush you can afford.

Airbrushes come in a variety of styles, frcm single action devices which have a simple trigger to turn the air flow on and off, with paint flow being controlled by a needle which is manually set by the modeller, to more complex double action airbrushes which generally have a system whereby pushing down on the trigger starts the airflow and then pulling back on the same trigger retracts the needle to allow paint to flow. There are siphon feed types where the paint is drawn up from a paint bottle below the brush and gravity feed types with a reservoir on top of the brush into which paint is placed, and some brushes are versatile enough to be either as the modeller demands. Some of the biggest names on the market these days are Badger, DeVilbis, Testors' Aztec, Harder & Steenbeck and Iwata. All of these manufacturers produce a wide variety of airbrushes to the very highest engineering standards, and can be relied upon.

Another thing to consider is an air supply – an airbrush needs air to function! For many modellers the starting point will be cans of compressed air. Whilst perfectly usable, there are limitations – the pressure will drop rapidly in use, limiting their effectiveness to minutes at a time, and all too often a modeller can find the air pressure running out or running low half way through a job, leaving a half painted model pending their next purchase of air, and worse yet, an airbrush filled with paint and no means to effectively clean it! Using cans of air will also work out very expensive very quickly.

For most people, however, the obvious

option is an air compressor. In days past a compressor was a major investment for a modeller, likely to be several times the cost of the actual airbrush. These days, with a ready supply of decent compressors coming in from the far east, a compressor can be obtained cheaply and quickly, and often will be cheaper than the actual airbrush. A simple piston type compressor will provide a constant, if inflexible air source. A little extra outlay will secure one with an air tank and pressure regulator and this will allow much greater versatility in modelling – a constant source of variable pressure air is the key to the art of airbrushing.

PREPARATION

One of the major differences between airbrushing and hand brushing is that an airbrush enables fine coats of well thinned, atomised paint to be sprayed onto the model, resulting in an even, silky smooth finish. Regardless of what kind of paint is used, either acrylic or oil based enamels, will all require a degree of thinning prior to spraying or the results at best will be a rough, gritty finish, at worst a clogged airbrush that needs stripping down and cleaning. These days some manufacturers do sell pre-thinned paint, but even these will often require a little extra thinner to spray well. While it is often preferable to use the manufacturer's own thinner, most enamels can be successfully thinned with turpentine or white spirit, available cheaply and in quantity from any D.I.Y. store. White spirit can also be used to spray through your airbrush to clean it after a spraying session.

Acrylics are very different, and there are major differences in formulation from manufacturer to manufacturer, and what will thin one paint will cause another to separate or even curdle and turn into a thick, glutinous mixture which will instantly clog an airbrush. The best advice where acrylics are concerned is to use, wherever possible, the manufacturer's own thinner, which will have been specially formulated to work with their brand of acrylic paint. For the most part, after spraying, acrylics can be cleaned

Fig 5.22 This compressor has a holding tank that cuts off the motor once the tank has been filled, and which kicks in only when it needs topping up. A pressure gauge allows the amount of air going to the airbrush to be varied, while a moisture trap stops water building up in the air line.

Fig 5.23 A more advanced model, this Iwata Revolution is a gravity-fed double-action airbrush that offers great precision and control.

out of the airbrush with either some more of the manufacturer's own thinner or a proprietary airbrush cleaner. What is vital is that an airbrush is thoroughly cleaned of paint after any spraying session, and especially in the case of acrylics, which can dry rock hard in a very short time and render an airbrush unusable without a very extensive strip down and clean out.

When it comes to preparing paint for spraying, many modellers will decant their paint straight into the glass jar if it is a siphon-fed airbrush or the colour cup if it is a gravity fed model. Add some thinner, thoroughly stirring the mixture, preferably with an old paintbrush. Many modellers feel

the ideal consistency for thinned paint is akin to skimmed milk but in reality if you pick up a drop of paint and place it on a vertical surface such as the inside of the colour cup it should run freely down the surface leaving a trail of paint. If it does this you can be reasonably certain that your mix is sprayable through most brushes. One of the great joys of airbrushing is how personal it is, and most modellers will develop their own techniques and procedures as they go – there are no hard and fast rules. Over a fairly short time you will simply develop a 'feel' for how your thinned paint will perform. Too thin and runny? Add some more paint. Too thick and clogging or going on roughly?

Add some more thinner. Some acrylics spray better if a couple of drops of retardant are added, as this helps prevent the paint from drying on the tip of the airbrush. If your air source has a variable pressure you should also feel free to experiment with varying the amount of air. Often a paint that seems too thick to spray well will begin to perform very nicely with a slight pressure increase, and vice versa – this is where a decent source of constant pressure will pay off, in allowing the modeller to experiment.

With your paint mixed and in your airbrush it's now time to actually apply it to your model. When spraying, one thing that will become apparent very quickly is that a little paint can go a very long way. The thinned paint and the good coverage of an airbrush means that you will use far less paint to achieve a good finish than you will with a traditional brush. Apply paint in smooth, even strokes to your model. Do not linger in any one place on the model, as paint can rapidly build up and start to run. If this happens don't panic, either allow it to dry off or use a paper towel moistened with thinner to remove the offending paint and reapply. Move your whole arm, resist the urge to move just the wrist and start and finish any paint stroke off the model. With something small like a 1:72 Spitfire you will find that you will cover the model in a matter of minutes with an airbrush, indeed, often you will spend more time preparing and then cleaning your airbrush than actually spraying the model! But the benefits of using an airbrush will become very clear in the quality and finesse of your paint coats.

AIRBRUSHING CAMOUFLAGE

In essence applying coats with an airbrush is no different to applying one with a paintbrush in terms of procedure. Work from light to dark, wait for one colour to dry before moving on to the next, and be patient. The major difference comes in applying things like camouflage colours. With increasing expertise many modellers will develop the skills necessary to freehand paint camouflage finishes with an airbrush using no masking techniques. But such techniques fall squarely into 'advanced' modelling. One very simple technique for masking and spraying a camouflage finish that is cheap, quick, easy and yields superb results is to use Blu-Tack to mask out the divisions between camouflage colours.

Take a piece of Blu-Tack and work it with your hands until it is warm and sticky, and then roll it into a fine sausage a few millimetres thick on a flat surface – something like a kitchen tile or piece of glass is perfect for this, but any clean, flat surface will do. Refer to the camouflage diagram provided with the model and use the Blu-Tack to mark out the division between the two camouflage colours. Work slowly and carefully, marking out the camouflage with the Blu-Tack. Do not hesitate to lift the Blu-Tack and try again if

Fig 5.24 Airbrushing camouflage freehand can be done, but it takes skill and practise. A simpler method is to use Blu-Tack to mask the pattern.

something doesn't look right when compared to the instructions.

With the camouflage marked out it is time to completely mask the areas to remain in the base colour. You can use liquid masking agents such as Humbrol's Maskol for this, or simply use pieces of masking tape cut to size and laid on the model. When this is done your model should now be completely masked apart from the areas intended to be painted the new colour.

Mix your second colour and then begin to apply in the same way as the base colours. Try to keep your airbrush at ninety

degrees to the surface you're spraying, and continue until you have covered the exposed areas completely. Once the colour is applied you can then remove all of the previous masking to expose your finished camouflage. What you should find you have created is a very subtle line between the two colours. The Blu-Tack will act as a slightly raised mask and create a very tight but very slightly blurred line between the camouflage colours, which looks extremely realistic. As before, be prepared to spend longer on the masking than on the spraying, but the work will be more than justified by

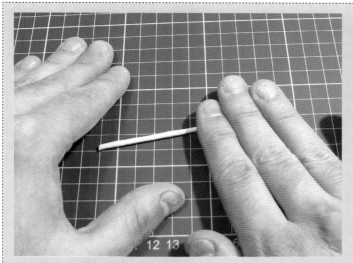

Fig 5.25 The Blu-Tack is kneaded and rolled out to produce "worms" than can be manipulated into shape more easily.

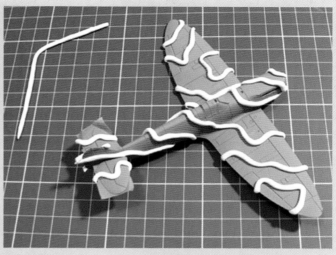

Fig 5.26 Keep referring to the kit's camouflage diagram; it may take some adjustment until the final pattern is achieved.

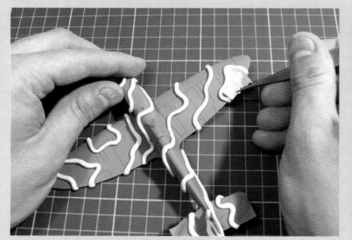

Fig 5.27 The remaining areas can be filled in with masking tape.

Fig 5.28 The dark green is airbrushed in light coats. Once dry, the masking is carefully removed, revealing a sharp-looking camouflage that retains slightly soft edges.

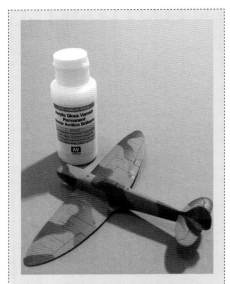

Fig 5.29 A coat of gloss varnish not only seals the paint finish, but prepares the model for decaling.

the finish achieved. Be prepared to go back over the model once dry to touch up any areas that have escaped the brush or look wrong – time spent here will be repaid with the finished article.

The rest of the procedure for completing an airbrushed model is essentially no different to a hand painted example. With the camouflage applied a gloss coat can be applied ready for the next step – decals.

CLEANING YOUR AIRBRUSH

Like caring for paintbrushes, airbrushes also need to be cleaned after use, particularly as they are precision instruments that will stop working if clogged with dried paint.

For gravity-fed airbrushes, decant any excess paint into a container and wipe the colour cup with a piece of tissue. Now apply a few drops of thinner into the colour cup and, using an old paintbrush, clean any paint still remaining in the feed channel and decant into a container. Now add some more thinner, this time spraying through the airbrush, until the thinner comes out clear. One trick is 'back flushing' where a finger is placed over the nozzle, causing the airflow to feed back upon itself and bubbles to appear in the colour cup (or paint jar). Suffice to say extreme care has to be taken so as not to splash thinner and paint onto the user. There are also commercial brands of airbrush cleaner that are essentially strong solvents that 'melt' the paint out of an airbrush – very effective, although these should be used with caution. With the airbrush clean, unscrew the needle and give it a quick wipe before carefully replacing.

For siphon-fed airbrushes simply replace the colour jar with one containing thinner and again spray through until the thinner comes out clear, then remove and clean the needle. Some companies sell cleaning stations which filter out all the vapours when spraying thinner and these are worth considering.

Should an airbrush become clogged then a strip down is inevitable. Nozzles can be soaked in solvent and the airbrush body flushed with cleaner and cleared using specialised reamers or even pipe cleaners. This can often be a messy and time consuming process, so the moral of the story is to avoid it by always following basic cleaning procedures immediately after painting.

Fig 5.30 Cleaning an airbrush is essential to maintain its precision performance.

Fig 5.31 Commercial airbrush cleaners can be used to flush the airbrush out, removing any paint still remaining.

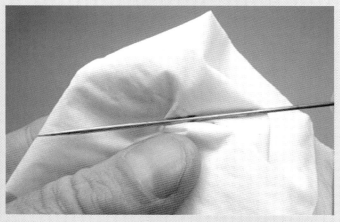

Fig 5.32 With the airbrush clean, the needle is given a wipe and then carefully replaced.

Step by step build 2 by Adam Cooper

1:76 German Panzer IV F2

1:76 AIRFIX PANZER IV F2

The Airfix kit of the famous WW2 German Panzer IV tank is an ideal subject for an introduction to small scale AFV modelling. The aim of this step-by-step build is not to provide details on how to super detail the kit, but to act as more of an illustration of some of the simple steps that can be carried out during construction to improve or personalise not only this, but any other military vehicle kit in any scale.

The Panzerkampfwagen IV first entered service with the German Army in 1936. Originally designed as an infantry support tank with a short barrelled 75mm gun, continual development incorporating the lessons learned in battle and more importantly arming with a more powerful longer barrelled gun ensured that the Panzer IV remained in production and on the frontline in all theatres that German forces operated. Despite the later introduction of the more powerful Panther and Tiger tanks the Panzer IV remained in service forming the backbone of the German armoured forces until the fall of Nazi

1.2

1.1

Germany in 1945. Even after the war later versions of the Panzer IV were used by Arab forces in the Middle East.

Airfix's 1:76 scale kit (A02308) of the Panzer IV was first released in 1971 and has been a mainstay of the kit range almost ever since. Comprising of 101 plastic parts and two vinyl tracks, a small decal sheet provides markings for two vehicles of the German Afrika Korps. Optional parts enable the construction of either the early short-barrelled 7.5cm Kw.K. L/24 armed Ausf F1 version or the later Ausf F2 variant fitted with the longer barrelled 7.5cm Kw.K 40 L/43 main gun. The overall dimensions of the kit are pretty good and it provides an inexpensive means of building this famous tank or providing the base for conversion or further detailing. **See Fig 1.1.**

Before construction check the kit parts to see if there are any flash, sink marks or the blemishes left by ejection pins from the moulding process. Cut these parts away from the sprues and deal with them using the techniques provided in earlier chapters of this book. **See Fig 1.2.**

The hull sides have prominent ejection pin marks between the suspension units that require filing or scraping away with a sharp knife. **See Fig 1.3**.

One aspect of modelling tanks that can make people rapidly lose interest is the cleaning up of the suspension wheels. Cutting carefully close to the kit part ensures a minimal amount of plastic is in need of removal. A foam-backed sanding stick is the best tool for removing any moulding 'pips' from the curved wheel and less likely to cause 'flat' areas if using a hard file. The drive sprockets require very careful removal so as not to cut off any of the teeth. **See Fig 1.4**.

As mentioned earlier in this book the test fitting of parts is not a stage to be skipped, especially if filler is required for any faults. Waiting for this to harden can hold up a build unnecessarily. On the Panzer IV there are some gaps where the turret parts join that require filling and sanding flat. **See Fig 1.5**.

The upper hull parts can also be fixed together and allowed to dry. **See Fig 1.6**.

The kit's exhaust (parts 86 and 87) were glued together and the prominent joint line cleaned up. To replicate the rough rusted surface of the exhaust, the kit part was held in a pair of locking tweezers and coated with a liberal layer of liquid glue. After leaving this for a short while to soften the plastic, the surface was stippled with the same hard stiff brush from the liquid glue, leaving the exhaust with a rough surface texture. This was then put aside to allow the surface to harden. **See Fig 1.7**.

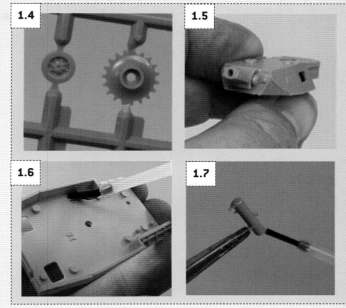

The rear idler wheel (parts 28,29,57,58) have some flash between their spokes so this was cut away with the point of a modelling knife and then cleaned up with a thin rat-tail file before gluing them together. **See Fig 1.8**.

Some vinyl tracks can cause problems when it comes to joining them together due to the nature of the soft plastic used that is impervious to normal plastic glue. Methods of joining them can include 'welding' them together with a hot screwdriver melting the joint pins, stapling with a mini stapler, gluing with special adhesives or even sewing them together! However care must be taken when trying to stretch the joined track around the wheels of the tank; if too tight the wheels can be weakened or snapped off altogether, causing further problems, e.g. having to repair the broken axles with metal pins. An alternative is to glue the track in position once it has been trimmed to the required length, using superglue, 2-part epoxy, PVA or silicone glue.

After cleaning up the drive sprocket teeth on parts 26, 27, 55 and 56 they were cemented together ensuring that the teeth on both sides of the sprocket are in alignment. Gluing the track onto the drive wheel at the same time can help ensure everything is lined up properly. Choose a suitable position on the tracks so that the later join of both track ends is where you will see it the least – either underneath the road wheels or mudguards. By test fitting and referring to photographs you can judge how much of the track should be glued onto the drive wheel and mark it accordingly. Use a bulldog clip or clothes peg to keep the track in place whilst the glue dries. **See Fig 1.9.**

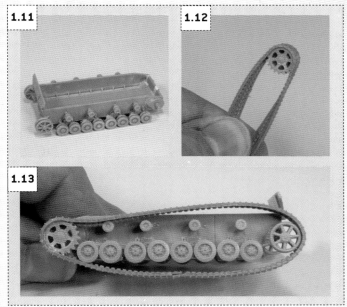

The lower hull components and the remaining suspension parts can now be attached to each other. **See Fig 1.10.**

Try to ensure that the hull sides are square and that the running gear is in alignment both horizontally and vertically. A short piece of 1cm square section wooden strip was used for this, taped down either side of the hull to prevent the suspension slowly splaying outwards under its own weight. Once aligned leave this assembly and the glued drive wheels and tracks to one side, preferably overnight, to fully harden. **See Fig 1.11.**

After drying, the drive sprockets and attached track assemblies can be fitted to the hull. **See Fig 1.12.**

In the Airfix kit the tracks are moulded slightly too long, so these are carefully trimmed a little at a time to the correct length. **See Fig 1.13.**

The tracks are then attached using the same preferred glue used to join them. Place this assembly on something flat, preferably

1.14

with a non-porous barrier such as polythene or kitchen foil to prevent the tracks being glued to the flat surface. The tracks can have a natural tendency to bow rather than lay flat, so placing 3 or 4 full tins of model paint on top of the hull will help weigh it down and ensure the road wheels are in contact with the tracks as the glue dries. When the glue has dried the construction of the lower hull and suspension is complete. **See Fig 1.14**.

The Airfix kit comes with separately moulded turret and hull hatches; apart from the two piece commander's cupola hatch the instructions only indicate that these should be glued in the closed position. To add some variety and personality to this model, the hatches were opened. As moulded, the hatches are very thick and look more like underwater pressure hatches or the door to a bank safe! **See Fig 1.15**. They were thinned down to a more scale appearance by filing and sanding. **See Fig 1.16**.

The two upper hull (part 78) hatch openings are far too small for a scale figure to climb through and require opening up with a sharp knife and file so that they match the size of the hatch doors. **See Fig 1.17**.

The turret side hatches are moulded as a single piece instead of in two parts and also have a large locating stub on the reverse.

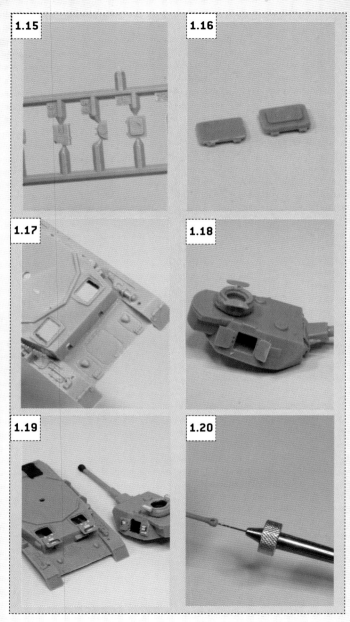

1.15

1.16

1.17

1.18

1.19

1.20

Before thinning these down test fit each door against the turret and draw around the hatch edge. You can see the amount of plastic on the turret that needs to be removed to make a more realistic opening. Using a flat or square shaped file and a sharp knife carefully enlarge the hatches to the inside edge of the door outline. Again using files and sandpaper, thin the hatch doors to a more scale appearance. When completed carefully cut the hatch into two parts using the engraved line on the outside surface as a guide, sand the cut edges flat again afterwards. As the hatch doors are different sizes it is a good idea to mark them in some way so that they do not get mixed up. By referring to pictures of the tank in use the hatch doors can be glued in their open positions. **See Fig 1.18**.

The insides of the hatches on the Panzer IV are not featureless flat plates of metal, they have all kinds of head cushions, hinges, handles, vents and periscope equipment which needs to be portrayed in some way to give a more realistic look. Again pictures can help with the detailing. Using scraps of plastic card and rod some of this detail can be replicated. **See Fig 1.19**.

A simple improvement to any tank kit is to drill out the end of the gun barrel. Dividing the gun size by the kit's scale will tell you the size of drill to use. In this instance it's a 75mm gun in 1:76 – 75 divided by 76 is 0.99mm, close enough to a standard 1mm drill bit. Use of something a little bit bigger such as a 1.5mm drill would result in an 'upgunned' model fitted with a 114mm gun - bigger than that of some modern tanks!

A small pilot hole is marked into the centre of the barrel end with a needle or sharp point of a knife to give the drill bit something to 'bite' into and prevents the bit from slipping or drilling off centre. If making the later, longer barrelled version included in the kit, the muzzle brake at the end of the barrel also requires 'cleaning' up, by sanding it to a more bulbous shape and opening the side vents by drilling through the flash and filing into shape with a small triangular rat-tail file. **See Fig 1.20**.

The upper and lower hull assemblies can now be glued together and any gaps filled and sanded. The on vehicle equipment can also

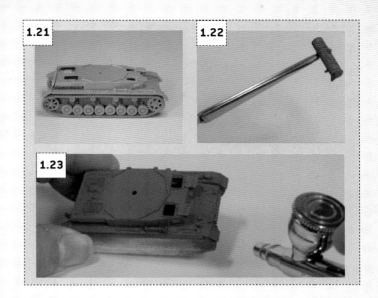

be added in preparation for the painting process.**See Fig 1.21**.

PAINTING

The exhaust muffler firstly requires the outlet pipe to drilled for a more realistic look, then painted to represent the burnt and rusted effect apparent on the real thing. An initial base coat of Brick Red H70 is applied, followed with a dry brushing of Leather H62. This highlights the rough texture applied earlier in the build. When dry a watercolour wash of red/brown can be applied in a dappled pattern, following this up with a slightly different shaded coat of watercolour. When dry, Black H33 can be dry brushed on for a sooty look around the exhaust pipe outlet. **See Fig 1.22**.

The entire lower hull, tracks wheels etc are painted Chocolate H98, over this a lightened mix of Chocolate H98 + Pale Stone H121 can be applied, and then a subsequent further lightened misted layer applied, replicating the dirty and dusty lower hull of a tank in service.

The wheels and tracks can then be masked off and the vehicle's

1.24

1.25

main camouflage colour of overall Tank Grey H67 applied in a couple of coats to the upper hull and turret. **See Fig 1.23**.

After the base colour has dried and the masking removed the final detail assembly and painting is carried out. This including adding the exhaust, and a thin plastic rod replacement barrel for the kit's oversize hull machine gun. Detail painting of the vehicle tools, wooden jacking block and the black hatch equipment can also be done using a variety of gun metal, brown and black paints.

A coat of gloss varnish, or a product such as Future Klear floor polish, is now applied in preparation for the decal application and detail washes. **See Fig 1.24**.

DECALS AND FINISHING

The decals can now be applied, leaving off the DAK palm tree insignia and sealed with another coat of gloss varnish. After allowing to dry, a dark grey (almost black) wash can be applied around the detail with a small brush. Unlike a matt surface where the wash can spread, the gloss surface helps control the effect - known as a 'pin wash' – adding 'depth' to the surface details. Any excess wash is wiped away with a cloth before allowing to dry, preferably overnight.

Further detail can be enhanced by dry brushing, using Sea Grey

H27 over the dark grey camouflage areas and a heavily lightened Chocolate over the suspension. Some light stippling with Tank Grey H67 over the suspension gives the impression of some areas having the dirt scuffed back to the basic camouflage colour.

The track detail, tools, machine guns and sprocket teeth can be highlighted with a very light dry brushing of Aluminium H56. A couple of light misted coats over the lower suspension and hull of heavily thinned Dark Earth H29 and an even thinner Light Earth H119 blends everything together and gives the vehicle a nice dusty look.

An overall coat of Matt Varnish or Humbrol's Matt Cote completes the model. **See Fig 1.25**.

To give the completed tank some sense of scale and bring it to life (and make use of those open hatches) some crew figures can be added. These were converted from the Airfix Luftwaffe Personnel Set and after some simple alternations all five crew members can be posed inside the hatch openings. **See Figs 1.26–1.30**.

1.26

1.27 **1.28** **1.29** **1.30**

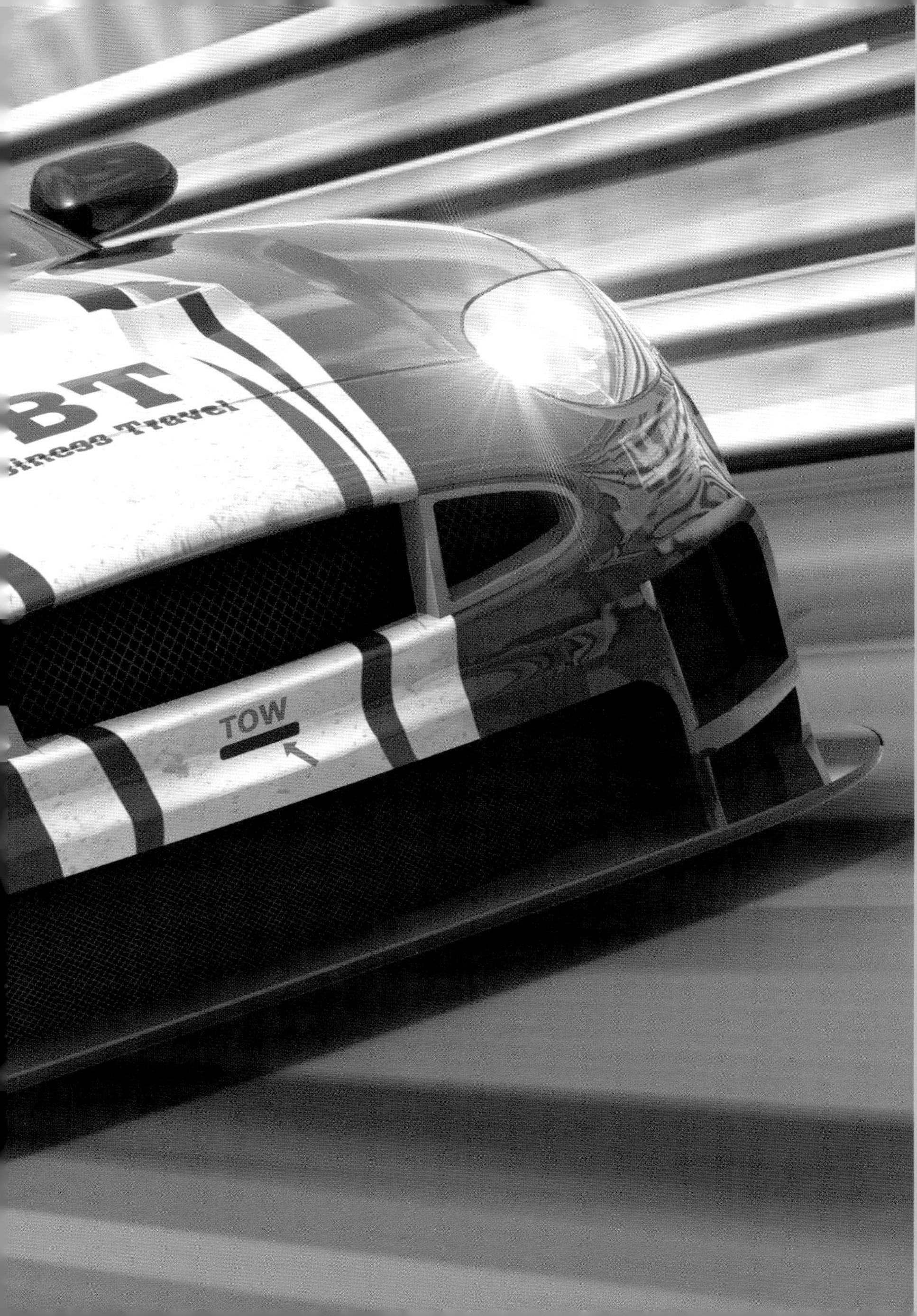

CHAPTER 6 Decals

DECALS

For many modellers, one of their favourite moments of the whole modelling process is when it is time to start applying the decals (or transfers). The first appearance of a few markings on a model really starts to bring the whole thing to life.

The vast majority of models these days come with waterslide decals for the markings. These consist of a design printed on paper containing a water-soluble adhesive, sealed with a varnish layer. When soaked in water the decals loosen from the backing sheet and can then be slid onto the model, with the (now wet) adhesive sticking the design to the surface of the model as it dries. It is a very simple process, and has remained basically unchanged for more than fifty years. The one thing that has changed is the quality of the decals. Even well into the 1970s a decal sheet would usually have no more than the main designs for a scheme on it, and any extra detail would have to be hand painted by the modeller.

From the 1970s onwards, increasing numbers of independent manufacturers produced decal sheets for models that were sold as enhancements to the model, offering the chance to finish a model differently to the decal options(s) supplied in the box. These were usually better researched and

Fig 6.1 Modeldecal set new standards for accuracy and attention to detail, not to mention the number of subjects included on each sheet.

more accurate than the kit decals, with many extras such as stencil and warning markings provided as well, and usually more extensive instructions on use and application. Perhaps the finest example of this was Modeldecal, produced by the legendary Dick Ward who also researched and produced decals for FROG, Matchbox, Revell and Airfix. Modeldecal's thoroughness and attention to detail raised the bar and are widely regarded as the benchmark even 40 years after they first arrived on the scene.

While Modeldecal only ever produced aircraft subjects, and exclusively in 1:72, Microscale in the USA had a range that not only encompassed aircraft in scale from 1:144 to 1:72, 1:48 and 1:32, but also military and railroad subjects, not to mention their own brand of decal products that created the 'Microscale system', a method that popularised the use of gloss and matt varnishes to hide decal film.

In more recent years the number of manufacturers and availability of aftermarket decals has exploded, with dozens and dozens of aftermarket manufacturers producing many hundreds of new sheets per year for modellers to use on their latest model. A knock on effect of this expansion in the aftermarket decal scene has been a vast improvement in the decals and instructions included in most kits these days, and vice versa.

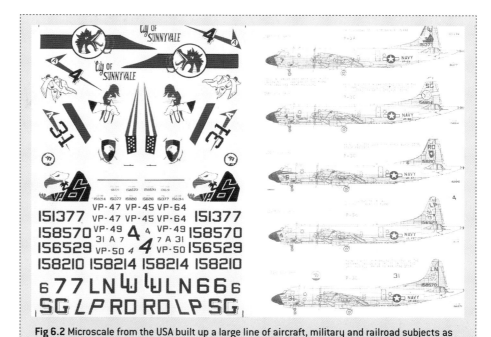

Fig 6.2 Microscale from the USA built up a large line of aircraft, military and railroad subjects as well as their own line of finishing products. This sheet covers P-3 Orions of the US Navy.

DECAL PREPARATION

Before beginning to apply the decals to the model some basic preparation is needed, which will yield far better results. Perhaps the most fundamental rule is that decals don't like matt surfaces. When a decal is applied to a matt painted finish, as it dries the irregular surface of the paint allows air to be trapped between the decal and the paint, allowing light to bounce off the surface and back up into the varnish covering – the result is an effect known as 'silvering', where the varnish becomes

visible. For best results a smooth glossy finish is required for decal application. Ironically, some model magazines in the 1960s would occasionally feature letters from modellers who found that decals stuck better to gloss-painted subjects like cars, trains and airliners, and that the varnish would disappear – military and aircraft modellers, meanwhile, would painstakingly trim the excess away until, one day, the penny dropped!

If you have used matt paints for your painting, once dry you can gently polish the

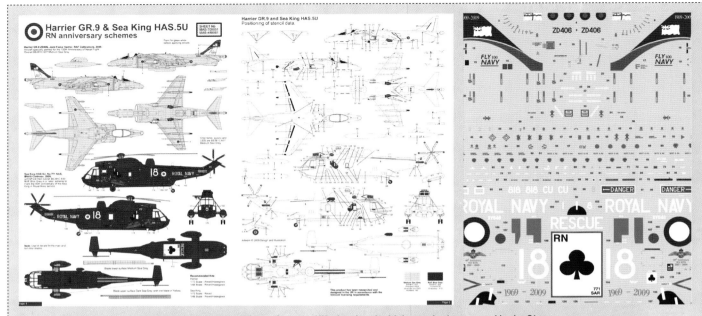

Fig 6.3 A modern day aftermarket sheet by Model Alliance from the UK, showing the high standards expected in the 21st century.

paint with a piece of cloth or kitchen towel. This will help to smooth the surface somewhat, but is unlikely to make it truly ready for decals. For best results a gloss coat is needed and these come in many different forms, from acrylic and enamel varnishes through to cellulose based lacquer finishes. Whilst the latter can yield the best, smoothest surface finishes they require great experience to use and certainly cannot be brush painted onto your model without risking a paint disaster!

One of the most popular and cheapest ways to achieve a gloss finish is to use household floor wax such as Pledge (formerly Johnson's Klear) in the UK and Future in the USA. This is available from most supermarkets, and will last a modeller years — indeed it is far more likely to need replacing due to it having gone off rather than having been used up. It is as thin as water, and using a wide, flat brush it takes seconds to apply a coat. The thinness of the wax means that one coat will rarely be enough to get a gloss finish, and very matt finishes will absorb initial coats and show little difference. This is normal, and the very rapid drying time means that you can add additional coats in a very short time to build to the gloss you require for decal application. When the final coat has been applied and has dried leave it to harden off, preferably overnight. It can then be given a final polish to bring out the shine.

WORKING WITH DECALS

Applying decals to a model is actually a very straightforward task, but certain techniques will repay a small investment in time and energy. Always take a few minutes to look at the finishing instructions and familiarise yourself with what needs to go where, and plan your application accordingly. Some decals may be multi part and require multiple levels of application, and the instructions will point these out. Some markings are partially obscured by other markings, for example a stencil may need to be applied over a roundel. A few minutes with the paint guide will highlight these issues and allow the modeller to prepare for them.

At its most basic, applying decals simply consists of soaking a decal in water until it slides freely around on its backing sheet and then sliding it into position on the model, then leaving it to dry. However there is much more that can be done do to help this process. The tools are simple – some warm water in a bowl or cup, fine scissors, tweezers and some tissue or absorbent cloth.

Warm water works best as it slightly softens the decal varnish, making the item more pliable, especially if positioning over raised surface detail. Also, a dash of washing up liquid or dishwater detergent helps cut down the surface tension and provides more of a lubricant in positioning the decal, thus reducing the risk of stretching or tearing.

Cut the individual design you wish to apply from the main decal sheet – taking care not to cut into the varnish surround – and dip it in the warm water for a few seconds. Don't worry if the sheet curls, this is normal and it will flatten back out as the

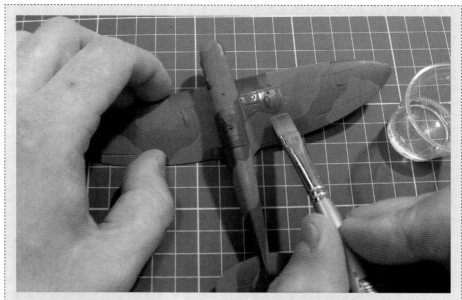

Fig 6.4 A gloss coat being applied by brush – it may take several coats to build up a smooth, glossy finish.

Fig 6.5 Alternatively a gloss coat can be airbrushed on, again being built up in light coats.

Fig 6.6 The basics needed for successful decaling – scissors, tweezers, a knife (for removing smaller items) and water.

Fig 6.7 Dip the decal in water for a few seconds then allow the water to soak into the paper and dissolve the adhesive backing.

Fig 6.8 The decal can then be applied using a brush or tweezers and floated into place.

water soaks into the paper. After 30 seconds or so the decal should move freely on the backing sheet. Using a soft brush slide the decal into position on the model, and once located accurately use a piece of tissue or cloth to remove the excess water. With the majority of the water removed you can now use the tissue to pad the decal down, and apply some quite firm pressure to get the decal to conform to detail and the surface of the model. This will help to seal the decal and minimise silvering as described earlier.

If you find that the decals are still silvering when dry, even on a gloss surface, then it could be that the decal adhesive isn't quite strong enough to make a bond. One

way to overcome this is to brush some more of the Pledge to the model, and while it is still wet apply the decal directly to it. As before, pad the decal down to remove excess liquid and then apply a thin coat of Pledge over the top. The Pledge should act as an adhesive and result in a decal that conforms perfectly to the model's surface, and shows no silvering at all – in fact many modellers use this technique as the cornerstone of obtaining a professional looking finish to their models.

DECAL SETTING SOLUTIONS

One of the best methods of ensuring decals settle down over heavy detail or

compound curves is the use of decal setting solutions like Micro-Sol and Micro-Set (the Microscale system), though most major accessory manufacturers have their own equivalents – such as Humbrol's Decalfix, Solvaset and Mr Mark Setter/Softer. These vary in composition and strength, but all basically do the same job.

With the Microscale system, the first part of the process is to use some Microset – this acts as a wetting agent that reduces the surface tension and allows the decal to be positioned more easily, as well as helping to eliminate air bubbles forming under the decal. Once in place let it settle for a few moments then pat down with a piece of tissue or cloth to remove any excess solution. The next step is to apply some Microsol which, as the name suggests, is a mild solvent. For those who have never used this kind of product before it can appear to have an alarming effect on the applied decal, softening and wrinkling it to the extent that it appears to be ruined – this is a normal part of the process! Resist the temptation to touch or smooth the decal down, as this will inevitably result in disaster as the softened varnish and ink is smudged or the decal is torn. Leave well alone and allow to dry – after a few hours the result should be a perfectly flat, very smooth decal with (hopefully) no silvering. Any bubbles or areas of silvering that remain can be treated by pricking the area with a sharp pin or needle and applying more of decal solvent. You may need

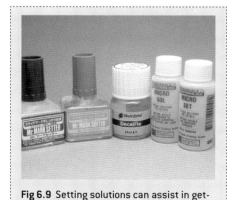

Fig 6.9 Setting solutions can assist in getting decals to conform to surface details.

multiple application on particularly recalcitrant decals, but the results should repay your patience and dedication with a very smoothly applied decal. This process pretty much applies to almost any of the kinds of decal products out there, save that some can be used as both a setting agent and solvent.

Once all your decals are on and dry, wipe the model with a moist tissue to remove any remaining adhesive that may leave a stain on the varnished surface and then apply a coat or two of the required varnish to seal them in and impart the model with the desired final finish.

The end result should be decals that have no obvious varnish or silvering and which appear to be 'painted on'.

TROUBLESHOOTING

Some decals may have an overly thick varnish coating which makes them especially stiff and reluctant to bed down. One trick is to soak them in slightly hotter water, which will soften the varnish somewhat, and the decal can then be applied using the processes already mentioned.

Another method is to lightly rub the surface of the sheet with a wad of Scotchbrite or similar, which removes a microscopic layer of varnish, slightly matting it in the process. This should be used with care as it is all too easy to weaken the decal and make it break up.

For some really obstinate decals,

brushing with a light coat of liquid cement will usually tame them – an extreme measure to be approached with care and caution so as not to ruin the painted finish.

On some rare occasions decals may break up either after being soaked in water or upon application – modellers with longer memories may remember the NOVO decals from the 1970s that often used to disintegrate upon contact with water. This may also occur with some decals in older kits where the varnish has become stiff and fragile over time.

The trick here is to carefully assemble the decal in place on the model (if possible) and touch up any gaps or cracks with paint. Forewarned with the knowledge that a sheet may cause problems, a couple of coats of varnish brushed on may solve the problem – if not, then it may be a case of looking around for aftermarket alternatives.

Another problem that may surface is decals that have yellowed, again because certain chemicals in the varnish may have deteriorated over time. This can sometimes be corrected by placing the decal in an airtight bag (a freezer bag for example) and taping to a window that gets sunlight – the ultra violet rays in the sun can bleach out the yellowing, but care has to be taken not to fade the whole decal. Also, be wary of any windows that attract condensation because you may find the decals have been removed from the backing sheet and applied to the window or bag by themselves!

DECAL ARCHIVE

One of the benefits of modern day kits is that they often include optional decals – by saving these, the modeller can quickly build up a collection of useful spares that can be adopted or adapted for other projects.

For example, a set of markings not needed for one modelling project may prove to be ideal for another, say a spare set of red/blue roundels to make a pre-war Spitfire Mk.I, or even adapting some USAAF markings to turn a Spitfire IX into an American-operated machine.

Even after a few modelling projects, a reasonable collection of spare decals can be acquired, and these can either be stored in an old kit box as a starting point, or separated out into loose A4 plastic sleeves and stored in a loose leaf folder. This is also an excellent way to store aftermarket sheets as it enables the decal and the instructions to be referenced very quickly.

For anyone interested in certain subjects and eras, for example WWII RAF, then an investment in some sheets of basic roundels and codes (like those made by Modeldecal or Xtradecal) is more than worthwhile, likewise for those interested in WWII Luftwaffe. In fact, with the latter, this is sometimes mandatory as the vast majority of, if not all, modern day kits do not contain swastikas (due to laws prohibiting their display in some countries). Thus, a sheet of aftermarket swastikas becomes a necessity if a model is to be finished accurately.

The general rule is never to throw anything away from a decal sheet. Even the borders that sometimes contain the decals can be adapted for wing walks, or chopped up to simulate stencils, shell ejector ports etc.

Decals can greatly enhance a model if properly applied, and the techniques needed are easy to master with simple care and patience.

WEATHERING

The art of weathering has become one of the more progressive aspects of the hobby in the last few decades as various new techniques and approaches have been pioneered, not to mention products to aid modellers. Whereas weathering was once seen as something of an afterthought – if a model was even weathered at all – many modellers now devote almost as much time to creating weathered looking finishes as they do in construction and painting.

But what is weathering? Simply put, it is the process of recreating the wear and tear seen on full size objects in miniature form. Mud, dust, rust, paint chipping, oil and water stains, all features often seen on real life machines, can be added to a model to create a greater sense of realism.

Perhaps the first modeller to really popularise weathering and turn it into an art form was Francois Verlinden from Belgium. His incredible dioramas and finishing techniques pretty much revolutionised the hobby for a generation, and his influence can still be found to this day in the methods modellers use to paint and weather their models.

In more recent years it is the work of the supremely talented Miguel Jimenez from Spain, and a new generation of talented young modellers who have created what is known as 'the Spanish school' of finishing. This is an approach which, while perhaps geared more towards the experienced modeller and a little outside the scope of a book aimed at the beginner, is worth seeking out, especially the instructional DVDs that demonstrate the techniques – they are truly inspirational.

Some modellers prefer to weather their model prior to decaling, some afterwards, the choice is entirely personal. There are many techniques for replicating weathering, using paints, brushes, pastel pencils, dry pigments and airbrushes. Most of the time it is all about what kind of effect you are after and using the best technique to suit, sometimes using a combination, other times perhaps one or two. The most important thing is to apply weathering logically rather than just slopping paint in a random fashion in the hope that it creates the right effect. There are reasons why areas on an aeroplane or tank get worn and dirty, and a study of full size examples in books and magazines – hence the importance of research discussed earlier – will show how and why this happens and will act as a guide.

Fig 6.10 This 1:72 Airfix Spitfire has been hand painted and decalled using the basic techniques described in the previous two chapters and shows how preparation and patience can produce excellent results.

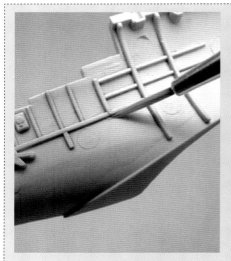

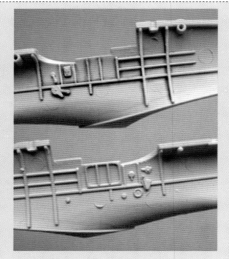

Fig 6.11 Using a fine pointed brush, a darker 'wash' is applied to run along the edges of the detail, emphasising the shadows.

Fig 6.12 The wash effect (top) compared to the basic paint finish.

In the case of an aeroplane it may be exhaust and gun stains, oil leaks and worn paint where the pilot and ground crew access the aircraft. With a tank it can be mud and dust around the tracks and running gear, oil spills across the engine decking or chipped paint revealing the original colour or primer underneath. Ships can benefit from rust streaks running down the hull and bridge – even cars can benefit from weathering, especially if recreating a rally car in its mud-spattered glory.

WASHES

Perhaps the two most-used techniques a modeller will use are application of a wash and drybrushing. Strictly speaking, both are artistic effects that, while not 100% accurate, do much to lift a model and create an illusion or impression of reality – ultimately a plastic model of a Sherman tank cannot be subjected to being driven through mud, water, splashed with oil and petrol or have big army boots thumping over the decking for months on end, so an impression has to be created. In fine art circles it is known as trompe l'oeil, which translates as 'to deceive the eye', which is sometimes what modelling is all about.

A wash is simply thinned paint or ink which is run into the panel detail, corners or recessed areas on a model during the painting stages. The effect is to darken the area and create some kind of contrast. The technique is especially effective on aircraft models that have recessed panel lines – the wash runs into the engraved details, making the panel lines stand out, mimicking how dirt gets trapped between panels on real aeroplanes.

Washes are also employed when painting the interiors of aircraft models and can add greater depth to, for example, a cockpit by intensifying shadows in the corners and edges of interior rib details, or the bezels and raised details on instrument panels and side consoles.

On AFVs and military subjects washes can be used to pick out panels, hatches and bolt heads, or to create the impression of oil spills from fuel cans – a model of a Sherman tank in desert colours will look more interesting once a wash has been applied to bring out the surface details and shadows in the light sand finish.

If overdone, a wash can make a model look toy like, but done with care and consideration for the final finish it can look excellent. Actual colours used for a wash can vary from dark greys to browns – black tends to look too stark – it all depends on the subject and what effect you are after. A brown wash on a tank can create the impression of rust accumulating in corners and look quite appropriate – the same wash

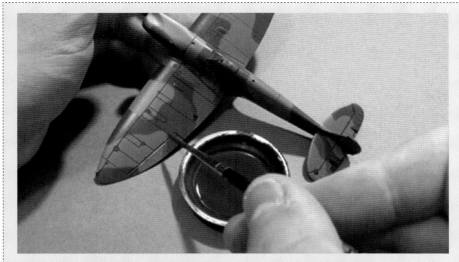

Fig 6.13 A wash being applied to pick out the recessed panel lines on this Spitfire.

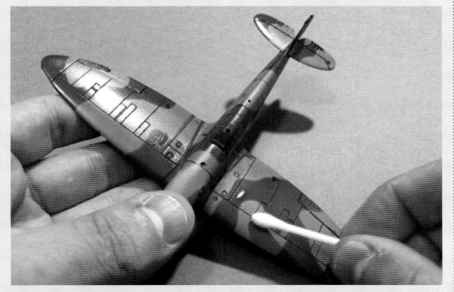

Fig 6.14 Any excess wash can be removed from the surface using a cotton swab.

on an aeroplane may look odd, making a serviceable machine look more like an abandoned rust bucket!

The intensity of a wash can not only be controlled by the amount of thinning, but also by adding a few drops of black or dark grey to the base colour to create subtle shifts in tone – it is all down to experimentation and personal preference.

The wash itself can be done with thinned enamel paint, artists' oils, acrylic paint mixed with water and some washing up liquid, or even some of the commercial brands of washes like those made by Vallejo. There are two approaches to applying a wash – a matt surface can help the wash spread slightly, creating a more blended appearance, whereas a gloss surface enables the wash to be tightly controlled and pinpointed, hence the phrase 'pin wash'. Using a small, pointed brush, apply a little of the wash and allow it to flow along panel lines or into the surface details. Any excess can be wiped away from the model's surface when the paint has dried, but not cured, with a tissue moistened in thinner or water (dependent on the paint type used).

Another approach is to lightly moisten the chosen area with a hint of thinner applied with a flat brush, and then apply the wash. The presence of thinner on the surface will help in controlling the wash and enable it to be blended if needed – but it goes without saying that the underlying but ensure that all coats of paint are thoroughly dry first.

DRYBRUSHING

While a wash adds shadows, drybrushing creates highlights. A paintbrush is lightly loaded with a slightly paler version of the base colour and the excess removed so that when it is brushed over a given surface, only the tiniest amount of pigment remains on the bristles, picking out the raised details and sharp edges. This is especially effective against darker colours, such as tanks and AFVs where drybrushing picks out rivets, bolt heads and hinges, and when used in conjunction with a wash creates more depth and interest to a model.

Items like exhaust pipes can benefit from being drybrushed in shades of browns and tans to create a hot, rusty look. The exhaust nozzles on a jet can be drybrushed using shades of gun metal and silver to impart a worn, metallic sheen.

Drybrushing the tread details on tyres or tank tracks with a sandy colour will give them a dusty look, contrasting with the darker base colours, while varying the shades can suggest different types of soils as well as fresh and dried dirt. Alternatively, tyres can be painted dark grey and drybrushed in black to give the impression of fresh, worn rubber. Figures can also benefit from drybrushing to bring out the folds and other details in uniforms and we'll look at them in a later chapter.

Fig 6.15 The hull of this Panzer IV has been painted grey, prior to drybrushing.

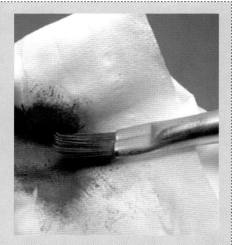

Fig 6.16 The key to successful drybrushing is to remove just enough paint from the brush.

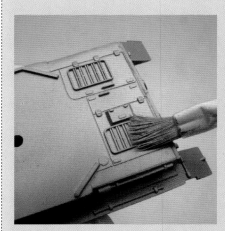

Fig 6.17 By using a paler colour, drybrushing helps highlight details.

Fig 6.18 Though exaggerated here for effect, drybrushing should be subtle, creating a suggestion of highlights rather than a 'frosty' look.

WEAR AND TEAR

Effects such as exhaust stains and cordite stains can also be achieved with enamel, oil or acrylic paint. Add a dab of the desired colour at the point where the stain is to begin and then leave it for a few minutes to begin drying. Now take a wide flat brush slightly moistened in thinner and drag it back over the paint in the direction you want the stain to go (e.g. back down the fuselage for an exhaust stain). The paint will be softened by the thinner and the soft bristles of the brush with pull it back over the finish creating a highly realistic stain, blending the edges into the paintwork. This can be repeated if necessary for heavier staining after the initial coat has dried, adding a touch of light grey closer to the exhaust pipes to suggest the decolourisation of the surface from the hot gases.

The same techniques can be used for oil and hydraulic leaks – for example, on the undersides of Spitfires there is usually a distinctive stain that starts around the carburettor intake and flows out towards the rear of the fuselage.

Another method for creating stains is using pastels, either obtained from an artist's set or using one of the pre-ground pigments (from brands such as MIG Productions and Vallejo) available from model shops. Use a soft brush or cotton bud to pick up some of the desired shade and apply it directly to the model in the direction

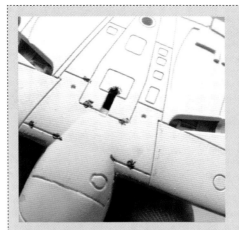

Fig 6.19 For the distinctive oil leaks seen on Spitfires, dots of black and brown oil paint were applied in key areas.

Fig 6.20 Using a soft, wide brush lightly moistened in thinner, the paint was streaked back, blending into the paintwork.

desired. Effects can be built up quickly with pastels, but it should be remembered that such finishes are quite fragile and won't stand up to handling very well. They do require sealing with a coat of, preferably sprayed, varnish.

Pastels and pigments can also be employed to create mud on military subjects, sometimes by mixing with an artists' texturing gel to create a lumpy finish that can be applied to the hull sides and running gear. Alternatively something as simple as talcum powder added to acrylic paint can create a rough mixture that can be used to simulate mud and dirt. There are also commercial products like Tamiya's Diorama Texture Paints that include soil, grit

and grass effects.

Paint chips can be rendered with a very fine brush and enamel or acrylic paint. Again, try to research your subject and apply the weathering as it would appear on the real thing. For example, paint is scratched on metal on areas like fasteners for engine cowlings, gun bays and also areas of heavy footfall such as wing roots. On a tank it will be along the edges and corners, areas crew use to access the vehicle, surfaces where external equipment is stored, or external areas that scrape against foliage or debris.

A very fine brush and thin paint are the key to success. While it is natural to use silver paint to simulate bare metal, the

Fig 6.21 Dry pigments or pastels can be used to simulate exhaust stains.

Fig 6.22 The mud on the back of the Sherman tank was created using acrylic paint and talcum powder, varying the colours to create different types of soils.

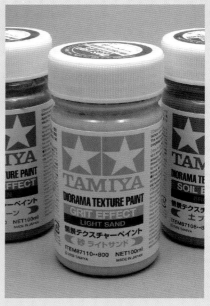

Fig 6.23 A new development from Tamiya are these Diorama Textured Paints, which can also be used for weathering.

effect can often look unconvincing as pure silver is too bright and appears to be sitting on the surface of the paint rather than giving the impression of being underneath it. Mixing a little light grey – or using grey itself – works better over darker camouflage colours. Conversely, on lighter colours, use a darker shade of grey – this works to great effect on subjects like German AFVs where vehicles had sand-yellow paint applied over the original panzer grey finish. Alternatively

the effect can simulate types of primers – edging the chip in a lighter colour gives the illusion of layers of paint. It's very important to work slowly and methodically with techniques like these, as it's all too easy to overdo such an effect.

Paint chipping can also be represented with silver artist's pencils (like Karismacolor) sharpened to a fine point and used carefully, but again some silvers can appear too bright and stark against darker

finishes so look for the more grey colours, using darker pencils on lighter base colours – experimentation is the key.

ADVANCED TECHNIQUES

Another recent innovation are filters, such as those sold by MIG Productions, which are essentially small amounts of paint suspended in a thinner that can be applied to simulate layers of dust and dirt, or to tone down camouflage colours by using varying tones similar to the base tones. Commercial filters do tend to be more expensive (around three times the price of a Humbrol tinlet) and take some practise to get the best results, so are perhaps slightly out of the scope of the beginner or intermediate modeller still getting to grips with the basics, but they are certainly something worth looking into and reading about.

As versatile as the airbrush is in creating high quality finishes, it can also be used for some subtle weathering effects. The most obvious is to simulate layers of dust with a light overspray of sand-coloured paint, usually after the decals have been applied. But perhaps the best technique that only the airbrush can create is what is known as pre-shading.

Essentially this technique involves applying the base coat (for example Sky on the underside of a Spitfire) as a starting point. A darker colour – usually black or dark grey – is then sprayed along the panel lines and control surfaces. It does not necessarily have to be fine or accurate, and the result may even end up looking a bit messy, but this is corrected by airbrushing another layer of the base coat, gradually reducing the starkness and blending the colours together. The finish effect should be a very subtle variation in surface tone rather than obvious sprayed lines.

A variation on this is to spray the model in the base colour, for example panzer grey on a tank, and then airbrush a slightly

Fig 6.24 Paint chipping on this Spitfire undercarriage door is applied using dark grey paint and a very fine pointed brush.

Fig 6.25 The effect of bare metal showing through worn paint can be created using pale grey paint and a fine brush.

Fig 6.26 An alternative approach is to use artist's pencils such as Karismacolor to depict worn metal and scratches.

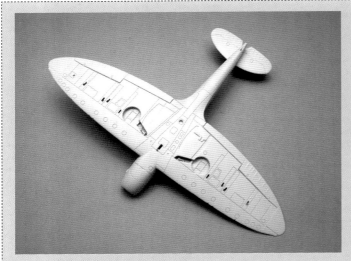

Fig 6.27 In preparation for pre-shading, a base coat of Humbrol 90 is applied to the undersides.

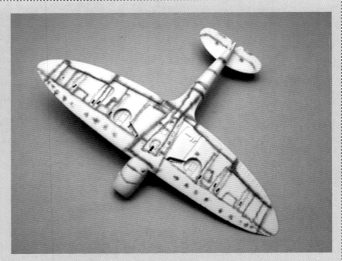

Fig 6.28 Thinned dark grey paint is sprayed over panel lines and control surfaces to create the pre-shading.

Fig 6.29 Another coat of Humbrol 90 is airbrushed over, slowly subduing the pre-shading effect.

Fig 6.30 The finished effect should be very subtle, suggesting a hint of shading rather than being too exaggerated.

Fig 6.31 The same 1:72 Airfix Spitfire as seen in previous pages, but finished using advanced techniques for painting and weathering. Skills to finish a model to this standard can be mastered over time, it just takes practise and the application of basic techniques to build up experience.

lighter mix into the centres of panels and surfaces, leaving the edges slightly darker, again creating a tonal variation that breaks up a monotonous colour.

One final trick that many modellers employ is to add a few drops of grey paint to matt varnish when applying a finishing coat. The grey slightly tones down the brightness of items like decals and helps tone all the colours together, creating a very slight, almost dusty finish, but one which is almost subliminal.

The key to all weathering effects is practice and experimentation. As mentioned earlier, even failed modelling projects can still serve a useful purpose as test beds for trying out new ideas and techniques. But once the basics have been mastered, weathering not only adds a great deal to the look of a finished model but can almost become an absorbing aspect of the hobby in itself.

Step by step build 3 by Brian Canell

1:32 Aston Martin DBR9

1:32 ASTON MARTIN DBR9

Between 1956 and 1977 Airfix have produced over forty 1:32 scale model cars. Many of these cars produced in model form were standard production cars that you might see on the road every day such as the Ford Escort or Morris Marina (this rare Airfix model kit can fetch nearly £100 on internet auction sites). One of the earliest kits Airfix released was a British race car that did rather well at Le Mans –the 1930 4.5Ltr Bentley. Now, nearly fifty five years later Airfix have released another legendary name in British motoring that has also done quite well on the famous French racetrack; the Aston Martin DBR9.

Although the DBR9 in many ways looks similar to the road going DB9 they are very different cars. The race car retains the chassis, 6.0ltr V12 engine block and cylinder heads of the DB9; almost everything else has been re-engineered for competition. Engine power has been increased from the DB9's 450bhp to around 600bhp on the DBR9. To reduce weight the bodywork (not including the roof) is constructed with carbon fibre. With a lightweight aerodynamic body this car can accelerate from 0–60mph in 3.4 seconds.

This build will show you how I made the Aston Martin. The kit comes as five sprues: the body shell, windows, and three sprues of car components.

BODY SHELL

The first step I did is to lightly sand down a moulding line on the rear quarter panels of the body. **See Fig 1.1**. After that the body shell is primed with white primer and then sprayed light blue – paint the front facia (bumper) now as well. The colour listed in the instructions is Sea Blue H47 which is the closest match in the range. To achieve a slightly more authentic colour you could add a very small amount of white (Gloss White H22) to lighten it up. Alternatively you could use automotive spray paint. A colour very near to Gulf's Powder Blue is

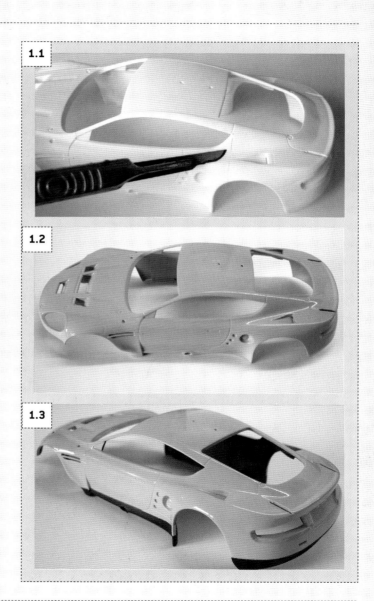

1.1

1.2

1.3

Ford Bermuda Light Blue, which is what I used. Using the aerosol give the model two or three light coats then leave for about half an hour. Now give the model a slightly thicker coat of paint so it looks wet on the body. It does take a little practise, but you want the paint to look wet enough to dry glossy but not too much so it runs. **See Fig 1.2.** A coat sprayed on too lightly can appear dull and misty looking.

Once the paint on the body shell had fully dried (a couple of days) it is masked, leaving the sills and the bottom portion of the rear valance, that is painted Matt Black H33. **See Fig 1.3.**

Now leave the body to one side for a few more days to let the paint harden completely. Sometimes automotive paint can feel dry but it is actually quite soft and it is easy to leave fingerprints in the paint.

CHASSIS AND BRAKES

The three main component sprues are then sprayed with primer. The wheels are sprayed Silver H11 as were the brake discs and the interior floor. **See Fig 1.4.** The final sprue is completely sprayed with Matt Black H33 as this includes the main floor pan, wheel arches, wiper, aerials and steering column. **See Fig 1.5.**

The wheel, brake and hub assemblies are painted before gluing. Note that on the DBR9 the rear wheels are larger than the front. The tyres are carefully hand painted matt black and it does take a steady hand not to get black paint on the wheel rims. When it comes to painting the brake discs paint the disc centres and the brake callipers Antique Bronze H171 to mak them stand out. The wheel hub mountings are painted silver and black. **See Fig 1.6.** The parts are all fitted together but be careful to make sure that the brake callipers are glued in opposite sides in the wheels because on the real car the brake callipers on each side face towards the centre of the car. Don't forget to scrape away the paint where the glue will be applied, in order for the glue to adhere properly. **See Fig 1.7.**

The wheel assemblies are glued to the floor pan and then the wheel arches are fitted. **See Figure 1.8.**

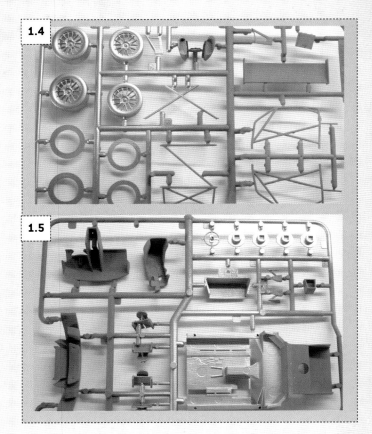

1.4

1.5

1.6

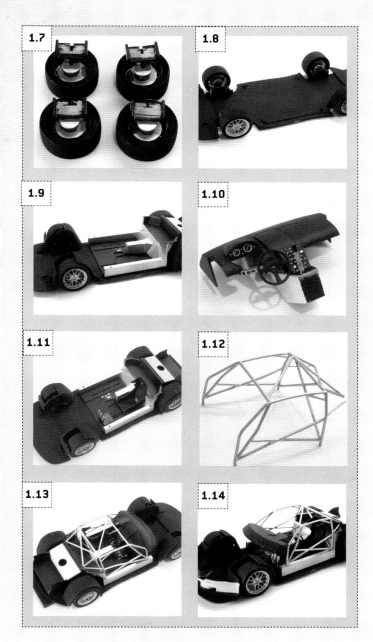

1.7

1.8

1.9

1.10

1.11

1.12

1.13

1.14

INTERIOR

Before the interior floor piece was added to the chassis detail it with some Semi Gloss Black H85 on the base. The stepped area and the rear interior panel with the hole is painted Semi Gloss White H130. **See Fig 1.9.**

The dashboard and instrument panel are next to assemble and paint. The dash is sprayed matt black and the switches on the centre console are picked out in silver and a little red, blue and yellow for the upper switches. **See Fig 1.10.** The driver's seat and pedal box are glued in place. **See Fig 1.11.** The four parts to the roll cage are painted Silver H11. **See Fig 1.12.** The dashboard and roll cage are then installed into the chassis. **See Fig 1.13.**

Before the front facia was fitted it is masked and the lower section painted Matt Black and the air intake area on the top of the part Semi Gloss Black. **See Figure 1.14.**

WINDOWS AND JOINING THE BODY TO CHASSIS

One thing I was keen to do when building this car was to replicate the gloss black window surrounds. Most modern cars have these, particularly on the windscreen and rear windows. My method is to stick the windows onto post-it notes and then draw a line around the windows. **See Fig 1.15.** Then, using small sharp scissors, carefully cut about 2mm inside of the line (leaving maybe 3–4mm on the bottom edge of the windscreen which would include the hole for the wiper) and re-stick the post-it notes back on the inside transparencies leaving an equal gap. **See Fig 1.16.** Then paint Semi Gloss Black H85 on the inside edges of the windows. **See Fig 1.17.** Once dry the post-it notes are removed and any errors or paint seepage can be cleaned up with a cocktail stick, as this will not scratch the clear parts. They are then fitted to the body shell. **See Fig 1.18.**

The tail lights are painted silver on the inside then Humbrol Clear Red H1321 on the lenses and finally a small amount of light blue for the inserts of the lamps. **See Fig 1.19.**

Just before the body is mated to the chassis the headlamps are fitted (Semi Gloss Black with Silver lamps). Putting the body shell

1.15

1.16

1.17

1.18

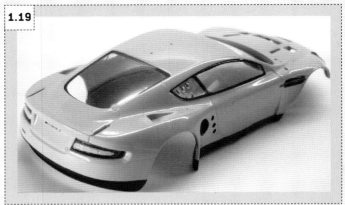

1.19

1.20

onto the chassis is straight-forward but it is quite a tight fit. It's now starting to look like a car! **See Fig 1.20.**

DECALING

Although there are many decals for this kit they are easy to apply. I notice a slight problem in that the front and rear orange stripes are a little short. They do not quite reach the radiator intake on the front and the rear does not go around the centre stop light. Touching in with some Orange H18 soon cures this. **See Figs 1.21 and 1.22.** It is easier to put the decals on the car before the rear spoiler, aerials, headlamp lenses, and mirrors are added. This is because the car will have a fair amount of handling and it would be easy to knock these parts off!

All done and ready to race! **See Fig 1.23.** This new tool of the DBR9 looks great with Airfix's other new car kit, the Jaguar XKR! **See Figs 1.24–1.25.**

1.21

1.22

1.23

1.24

1.25

A Tooby

CONVERSIONS

With a few models built straight from the box it's perfectly natural that the enthusiastic modeller should start to add some variety to their models. This may be something as simple as trying a new colour scheme by employing one of the countless aftermarket decal sheets available for nearly any subject, to some detailing work either using scrap plastic and plasticard or an aftermarket detailing/upgrade set.

Today's generation of modellers really are experiencing a golden age as far as aftermarket accessories are concerned. Thirty years ago the scope was limited to a few third-party decal sheets and a few, sometimes crude, vac-form conversions – the modeller was more or less on their own if they wanted to represent something out of the ordinary. This started to change in the early 1980s with the rise of the 'cottage industry' companies such as Aeroclub and PP Aeroparts in the UK who offered white metal and etched brass accessories that introduced many plastic modellers to the concept of mixed-media parts. Since then the aftermarket sector has exploded, and a quick look around any of the popular online modelling web sites these days will unearth countless conversions and detailing sets. For the most part these are either in etched brass or resin and in the hands of

Fig 7.1 A step up – PP Aeroparts from England were amongst the pioneers of aftermarket accessories in the 1980s.

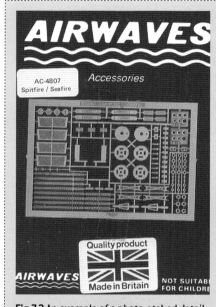

Fig 7.2 An example of a photo-etched detail set showing the kind of detail than can be produced using this process.

experienced modellers they can certainly raise a fairly basic model to a whole new level.

But that's not to say conversions and detailing are not within the scope of the beginner, far from it, and some very simple do-it-yourself exercises can not only radically change the look of a basic model, they can raise skill levels and build

experience towards trying out the more specialised aftermarket accessories.

Perhaps the simplest type of conversion is a change of colour scheme and markings using an aftermarket decal sheet, for example the Airfix 1:72 Spitfire Mk.I which can be built as per the instructions but finished as another aircraft

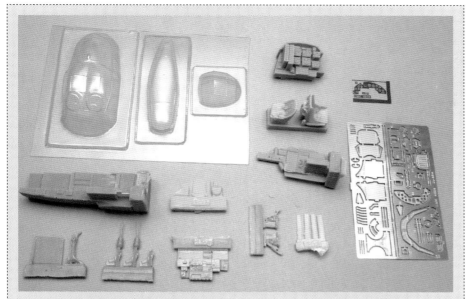

Fig 7.3 A 1:48 Junkers Ju 88 detail set by CMK from the Czech Republic that combines vac-form, resin and photo etched parts as well as printed film for the instruments.

Fig 7.4 An example of a simple conversion. This 1:72 Airfix Spitfire IX has had the wingtips sawn off and sanded to shape to depict a post-war French variant.

from the Battle of Britain using a third-party decal sheet. And for Spitfire, read Hurricane, Messerschmitt Bf109, Hawk, Harrier etc...

But in terms of a physical change to a model, this usually means something like cutting open the flaps or altering the angle of control surfaces of an aeroplane. Chopping the wing tips off the Airfix Spitfire IX can turn the model into a clipped-wing version. Swapping the De Havilland and Rotol propellers between a Spitfire and Hurricane can depict the alternate units both used.

'Kitbashing' is where two kits are used

to make one model, for example combining the fuselage of the Airfix 1:48 Spitfire XII with the wings from the Seafire XVIII as the starting point for a Seafire XV. While this may seem profligate, the resultant spare parts will be useful for other modelling projects.

The aftermarket scene offers parts to carry out all manner of conversions from simply replacing the nose of an aeroplane or the turret of a tank, to large and complex (not to mention expensive) sets where large parts of a kit are replaced, often requiring major cutting and altering of kit parts.

SPITFIRE PR.1G CONVERSION

A relatively simple conversion to try out on a basic kit is modifying the 1:72 Airfix Spitfire Mk.I to represent the PR.1G, one of the various photographic reconnaissance (PR) versions made during WWII. The work is little more than adding some camera ports and a new canopy, not to mention a radically different colour scheme, but all within the scope of a modeller who has put together a few kits.

Perhaps the easiest improvement that can be added to any kit cockpit is to make some seat straps using thin strips of masking tape. The natural tan colour of the tape is a near enough match for the canvas straps of the real thing and can be enhanced by adding some dots of silver for the buckles – as skills progress, the modeller can move on to specialised photo etched sets for seat belts, and even separate buckles in the larger scales.

The PR.IG featured three camera ports, one positioned on the port side radio hatch (behind the canopy) and the other two on the underside of the fuselage just aft of the wing trailing edge. Simply mark the locations of the camera ports on the fuselage radio hatch and under wing piece, and then drill and ream them out using a selection of files to a diameter of around 3mm. Once done these can be simply backed with small pieces of plastic sheet, to be painted and glazed at the end of construction, though more advanced modellers may like to build some interior and scratch build the cameras before glazing the camera ports.

The PR.IG had a canopy with two bulged, teardrop-shaped blisters on each side to enhance pilot visibility, but unlike later PR Spitfires that had a frameless windscreen, this version retained the framed and armoured windscreen (and full armament as well). The canopy is really the only major aftermarket expense specific to this model and can be obtained as a vac-formed item either from Aeroclub in the UK or Falcon in New Zealand.

For the PR.1G, the conversion combines the windscreen from the kit and the centre section of the vac-formed canopy, requiring each to be carefully cut apart. The centre section from the Airfix canopy was removed using a razor saw, leaving the windscreen and rear sections which had their edges

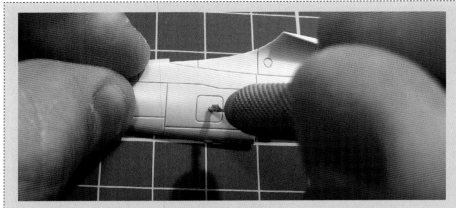

Fig 7.5 The fuselage camera port for this PR.1G conversion is marked and then drilled out.

Fig 7.6 The hole is opened out and further refined using needle files.

cleaned up with a sharp knife. The vac-form canopy was carefully cut and trimmed from the backing sheet using a pair of nail scissors. As the vac-form canopy is not made for this kit, the fit was less than ideal. This was disguised by posing it open to hide the mismatch. Alternatively the kit canopy can be used unmodified, but the blisters cut away from the vac-form canopy and fixed in place using white glue – though in truth, this is more tricky and potentially messy. The rest of the model can be assembled as per the kit instructions, then primed and prepared for painting.

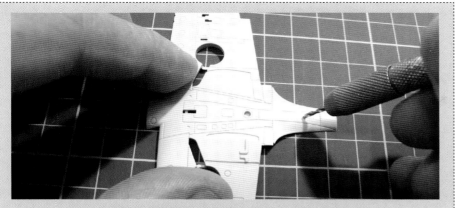

Fig 7.7 The camera ports for the underside are similarly drilled and opened out.

Fig 7.9 The kit canopy is sawn into three sections, retaining the windscreen and rear portion.

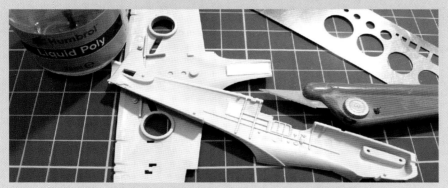

Fig 7.8 The holes can be simply blanked off with plastic sheet.

Fig 7.10 The centre section (with the teardrop blisters) of this vac-form canopy, by Falcon from New Zealand, is cut away using fine scissors.

THINK PINK!

Wher it comes to the final colour scheme fcr the PR.IG, it is about as different to the familiar camouflaged Battle of Britain Spitfire as it's possible to get – this one is pink! During WWII numerous RAF reconnaissance aircraft were painted in various shades of pink for use on missions at dusk or dawn. Arguments have raged for many years over exactly what shade of pink they were, from a deep pink to a slightly tinted white. A good compromise is to slightly tint a portion of white paint with some red to give a definite, but not overly strong, pink.

The pink is applied in several thin coats

to get a good overall coverage and then allowed to dry. Some weathering can be applied using the techniques already outlined, to simulate the exhaust stains on the nose and the usual oil smears on the undersides aft of the carburettor intake. To ensure a convincing finish, keep the weathering more on the subtle side than would be required for the usual camouflage scheme.

The model is then gloss varnished ready for the decals – markings for this scheme can be found on Almark Sheet A36 or can be assembled from generic sheets of RAF roundels, codes and serials, with the stencil and gun port markings coming from the kit. One oddity of this particular aircraft were the roundels, which were positioned inboard, close to the wing root. The decals are applied using the techniques mentioned in the previous chapter and, once dry, a finishing coat of matt varnish can be applied, though with PR aircraft a slight sheen may be preferable by adding a touch of gloss into the matt mix.

The only job left now is to finish the camera ports. As previously mentioned these were simply backed with sheet and painted matt black. The glazing can be added using various techniques from Humbrol Clear Fix to PVA glue or even two part epoxy glue. All will dry to a clear, glassy finish which can be further enhanced with a drop of gloss varnish.

The finished model, in its striking pink

Fig 7.11 The model is given a coat of pink, custom mixed using white with a dash of red, followed by gloss varnish.

Fig 7.12 The camera ports were touched up using black paint.

scheme, provides a stark contrast to the standard Battle of Britain version. Simple conversions like this add unusual models to a collection as well as assisting in building up skills and experience. Again, there is no substitute for practise, patience and perseverance.

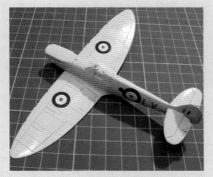

Fig 7.13 The decals came from various after-market sheets.

Fig 7.14 The camera ports were glazed using a two-part epoxy glue.

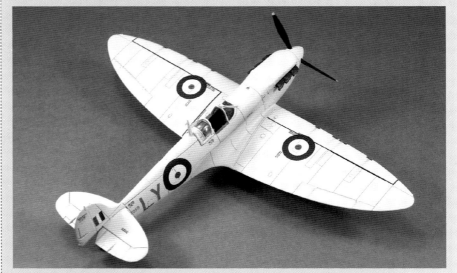

Fig 7.15 & Fig 7.16 The finished model in its unusual colour scheme is significantly different to the more familiar camouflage version, but the work required to produce it is relatively simple.

AIRFIX®

ROYAL NAVY

1:350 TRAFALGAR CLASS SUBMARINE

A03260 · MODEL KIT · MAQUETTE A MONTER · MODELLBAUSATZ · MODELLO A SCALA · BOUWMODEL · MAQUETA PARA MONTAR · PLASTBYGGSATS · RAKENNUSSARJA · MODELO PARA CONSTRUIR · MODELBYGGESÆT · ΣΥΝΑΡΜΟΛΟΓΟΥΜΕΝΟ ΜΟΝΤΕΛΟ

Step by step build 4 by Adam Cooper

1:350 Trafalgar class submarine

1:350 AIRFIX TRAFALGAR CLASS SUBMARINE

Released in 2010, the Airfix 1:350 Trafalgar class submarine is available in two versions – the standard kit (A03260) and a Royal Navy gift set (A50021) that includes paints and glue – the plastic parts are exactly the same for both releases. This newly tooled kit comprises 41 parts and builds to a model length of 245mm. The model is of the 'full hull' type complete with a display stand. Optional parts and decals enable one of seven T-class submarines to be completed. **See Fig 1.1.**

A change to the kit's full hull display is to create a realistic 'at sea' setting. The box illustration gives a pretty good idea of just how much of the submarine is visible above water. Additional reference pictures can be found in reference books and of course the internet. An inexpensive picture frame was acquired for the display base, along with some foam board from an art supplier and some acrylic sealant.

The main components are carefully removed from the sprues. **See Fig 1.2.**

This being a 'waterline' model, only a few of the kit's parts will be required – these parts are marked on the plastic sprues with red pen. **See Fig 1.3.** Due to their fragility and small size the periscopes and sensors were painted in situ.

The conning tower was made up as per the kit instructions and attached to the upper hull along with the upper rudder. With reference to the box art a line is drawn on the hull that indicates the 'waterline' of the sub. Although only the upper hull part is being used this highlights the need to 'submerge' the upper hull into the display base. **See Fig 1.4.**

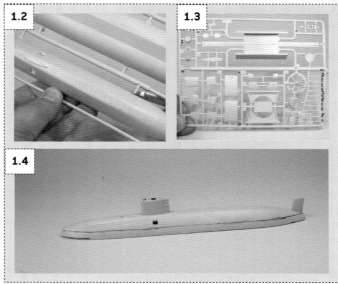

Art board is a lightweight thin polystyrene sheet sandwiched between smooth white cardboard and is readily available from art suppliers and craft shops.

An A4 sheet was cut to fit the frame and is used as the base. The outline of the hull is traced and then cut out, slightly oversize in order to ease the gluing of the hull to the base later on. **See Fig 1.5.**

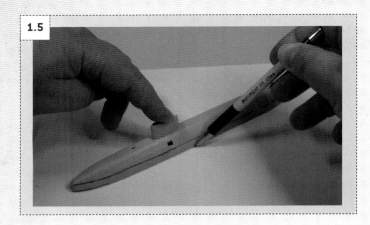

1.5

1.6

Card glued underneath the cutout provides support for the sub's hull. The base, frame and hull are then test fitted. **See Fig 1.6**.

There are a couple of sink marks on the two hull vents, parts 31B & 32B; these will require filling and sanding smooth before attaching to the hull along with part 34B. **See Fig 1.7**.

PAINTING

The exterior of most modern submarines are covered in a mosaic of rubber-like anechoic tiles, a form of underwater stealth technology that absorbs underwater sonar signals to hide or mask the sonar signature of the vessel. This is nothing new, the German Navy during WWII pioneered the use of this idea to fool Allied sub hunters. The use of these tiles causes a patchwork effect to the external appearance of the submarine and looking at the box art it can be seen that there are several shades of dark grey and black visible along with a few missing tiles, rust streaks and the hull markings. This weathered appearance can be replicated by applying varying shades of dark grey paint with different areas masked off in a random manner with small squares of masking tape.

After washing the hull in mild soapy water to remove any grease from earlier handling, the main hull is painted overall in Humbrol Matt Black H33, This will replicate the areas of missing tiles that appear as very dark areas in photographs. **See Fig 1.8**.

Once this coat of paint has dried, small 3–4mm squares of low tack masking tape can be applied in a random pattern over the model. As these masked areas will be the darkest areas of missing tiles only a few need to be applied. Reference to photographs shows that, as well as individual tiles being missing, sometimes a row or even a small block of tiles can come away from the hull. **See Fig 1.9**.

When the masking is complete the first of several thin coats of varying shades of dark grey paint is applied. **See Fig 1.10**.

When each colour has dried more masking tape tiles are applied, building up a patchwork of overlaid individual tile masks and some larger area masks, all the time ensuring that the edges of the masks are in line with those laid down already. **See Fig 1.11**.

This process is then repeated with different shades of dark grey, such as Tank Grey H67, Dark Grey H32, Sea Grey H27 or by adding varying amounts of 33 Black or 34 White to vary the shade. The lightest grey used is Sea Grey H27. **See Fig 1.12**.

Repeat this process until about five or six layers of dark grey paint and tile masks have been applied. After leaving to fully dry, the masks; can be carefully removed to reveal the desired patchwork effect. Be careful not to 'scratch' the paint surface when removing the masks, carefully using the end of a pointed scalpel blade aids the small mask removal.

1.7

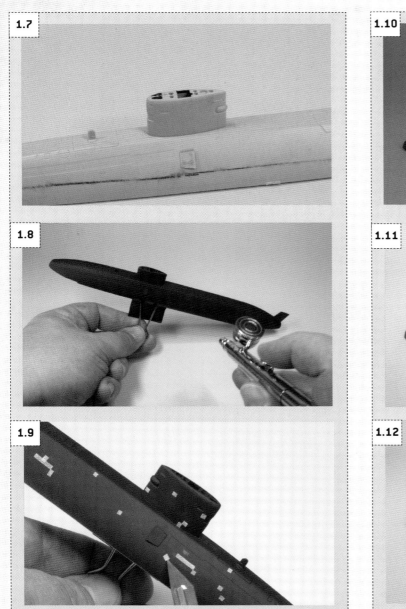

1.8

1.9

1.10

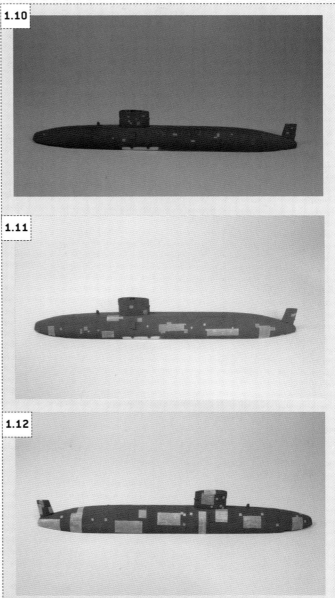

1.11

1.12

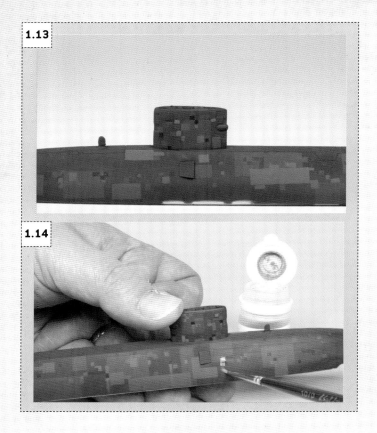

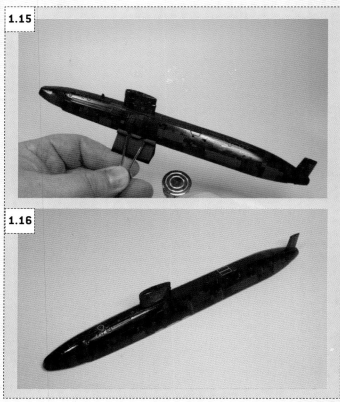

Once all the masks have been removed a patchwork sub should be revealed. The difference in the greys may seem a bit harsh at first, but later gloss varnish coats will reduce the contrast. **See Fig 1.13**.

FINISHING

Rust streaks can be applied by carefully masking below some of the 'missing' tile (black) areas and streaking in a downwards motion some suitably thinned rust coloured paint or a rust coloured weathering powder. **See Fig 1.14**.

Once completed, the whole effect can be sealed with a coat of gloss varnish, which will act as a leveller for the paint surface as well as providing a suitably glossy surface for applying the decals. **See Fig 1.15**.

If weathering powders were used for the rust staining then a sprayed coat of varnish should be applied – this will not smear the applied powder and ruin the effect. Once the gloss coat has hardened the decals can be applied using Humbrol Decalfix to help them shrink down over the moulded detail and give the decals a painted-on look.

Once dried they can then be sealed in with another coat of gloss varnish. This will provide a nice smooth 'easy wipe' surface in case of any accidents whilst applying the acrylic 'sea' to the base later on. **See Fig 1.16**.

Depending on the thickness of your display base surround an

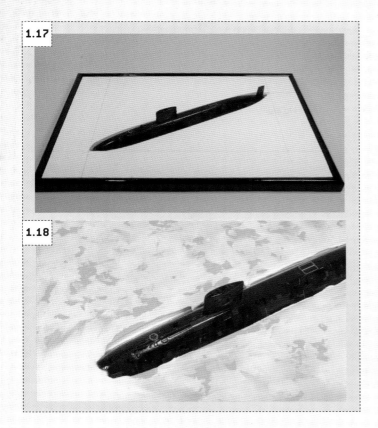

1.17

1.18

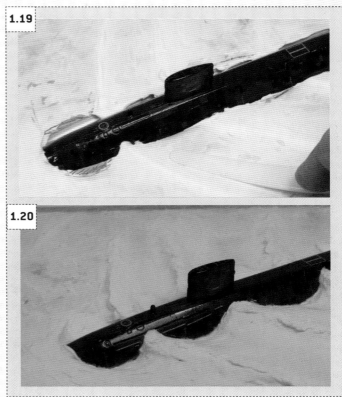

1.19

1.20

additional layer of art board may be required to bring the level of the base nearer to the level of the waterline. **See Fig 1.17**.

The painted hull can now be glued into position using PVA wood glue, silicon sealant or a two-part epoxy type glue.

MAKING A SEASCAPE

The artificial sea can now start to be laid down by randomly placing small blobs of preferably white acrylic (NOT Silicone) sealant over the flat surface. Using a palette knife, the blobs are flattened out to spread the sealant over the base. Gradually a random rippled look should start to appear. By angling the spreading action small

wave like shapes can be formed. Small amounts of water can be used sparingly to smooth out any jagged or lumpy areas. If you are not happy it can be scraped off and re-applied before it starts to dry out. The bow wave and the churned water at the stern can start to be built up gradually. This whole process takes a few days as the acrylic sealant needs to dry out between applications – it's not a case of spreading it out all in one session. **See Fig 1.18**.

The larger waves created by the submarine as it sails at speed through the sea can be formed by squeezing a thicker bead of sealant, and then shaping the wave with the palette knife. A gently smoothed slope behind the wave and the frothing crest at the front of the wave can be sculpted into shape with the knife or a wet paintbrush. Due to the thick texture of the material the distinctive folding over itself look of a wave can be created. **See Fig 1.19**.

The wave troughs can be created by cutting away the art board as required and then smoothing the sealant over these depressions. The sealant can be pushed up against the hull of the submarine either with a wet paintbrush or a water soaked cotton bud. Any excess can be wiped off the smooth glossy hull. **See Fig 1.20**.

The completed seascape is left to dry for a couple of days prior to painting. **See Fig 1.21**.

Using some inexpensive satin finish acrylic paints from a craft shop a suitable sea colour is mixed and applied to the sea base leaving a white outline near the hull and the sub's wake.

By gradually adding more and more white to this base colour and applying over the waves and near the sub the effect of the frothy water is created. After allowing it to dry, pure white is used for the wave edges and the turbulent frothy water closest to the hull. The areas where water is flowing over the hull is created by spreading and shaping a rippled layer of thick Artist's Gel Medium. When applied this is like a very thick white PVA glue, but it dries to an almost clear gloss while retaining its rippled shape. The ripples are dry brushed with pure white to accentuate them. Again any slips of the paintbrush on the hull can be wiped away with a wet cotton bud. After dry brushing and final highlighting with pure white the base is left to dry. **See Fig 1.22**.

The last stage is to cement to the conning tower the periscopes, aerials and sensors. Not all of these would be deployed at the same time so a selection is made after looking at reference photos. Areas of the hull that wouldn't have been swamped in water are painted with Satin Varnish H135 to tone down the gloss coat previously applied.

The model and its display base are now complete. A fairly simple project that would be ideal as a first attempt at a diorama. The same sea making techniques can be used with any model of a waterborne craft or indeed any seaplane or flying boat that you may wish to be displayed in an 'in action' setting. **See Figs 1.23–1.27**.

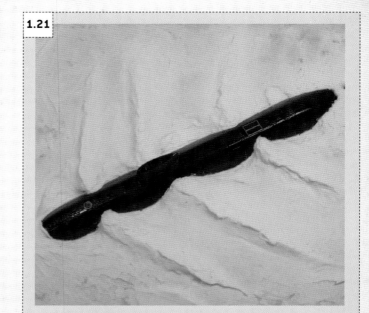

1.21

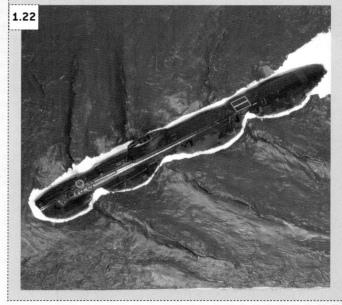

1.22

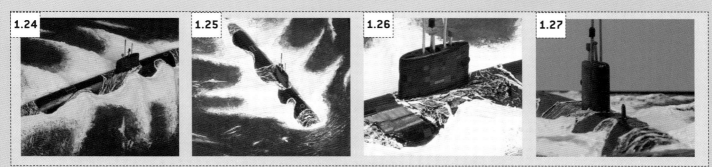

FIGURES

The art of figure painting is a hobby in itself and could easily fill up a whole book detailing the various kits, tools, techniques and paints available. Styles and philosophies vary from basic drybrush and wash techniques to a very 'painterly' approach where shadows and highlights are accentuated – all are equally valid and just depend on the kind of finish the individual modeller wishes to achieve.

The variety of kits to choose from is vast, both in terms of subject matter and scale. At the basic end of the market there are the kind of multi-figure sets made by Airfix, Revell and Italeri, through to kits produced using regular injection moulded polystyrene, cast white metal, resin, polythene and 'blown' vinyl. You can buy full figure kits or head and shoulder 'busts', everything from Roman soldiers to Starship Troopers, depending on whether your tastes tend towards fact or fiction.

METAL

The first commercial cast-metal figures go back to the 18th century and were moulded in metals like lead, primarily because metal casting was about the only mass-production method available. Even when plastic kits were becoming the norm, many of the niche companies specialising in

Fig 8.1 The high standard that can be achieved with figure painting. This is The Doctor and Martha from the Airfix Doctor Who 'Welcome Aboard' kit.

figures continued using metal-casting – the relatively low start-up costs, ease of production and cost-effectiveness (a reject figure can simply be melted down and used again), not to mention their ability to capture fine detail, remains popular to this day although non-toxic white metals have replaced lead.

Many figure modellers still prefer the solidity of working with cast-metal kits, cleaning up mould-lines is much the same as for plastic, though a good set of metal needle files works better than sanding sticks. While some opt for soldering parts together, they can equally be assembled using epoxy resin adhesive or superglue.

RESIN

Resin figures started to become more commercially available in the 1980s, mainly due to the pioneering work of François Verlinden who began perfecting better methods for resin casting on a larger scale. The advantage of resin over metal is primarily that it is lighter, so larger items can be moulded, but care has to be taken during the production process to ensure that air bubbles do not mar the castings. Vacuum chambers can help in minimising these but are expensive start-up costs and thus add to the price of the finished item. The disadvantage of resin over metal casting is that any reject moulding cannot be recycled.

Resin kits can be worked pretty much

the same way as plastic; the only difference is that resin is impervious to regular model glues, but works fine with epoxy and superglue.

PLASTIC

The first injection moulded polystyrene figures were the large scale kits made by Airfix and Aurora, mainly single personalities or historical figures like monarchs or knights. As mentioned previously, it was Historex from France who brought plastics into the more traditional 54mm figure market with their fine range of Napoleonic kits. Airfix followed suit with their 54mm Collectors Series and Multipose sets, but it was the arrival of Tamiya and their rapidly expanding range of 1:35 kits that saw polystyrene figures begin to become the norm, especially for WWII subjects.

POLYETHYLENE AND K-RESIN

Many modellers will have had their first experiences of model figures with the 1:76 or 1:32 sets made by Airfix, Matchbox, Italeri and Revell. These were moulded in low-density polyethylene, a soft plastic with a high rubber content. The flexibility of the polyethylene meant that parts could be moulded in a single piece with undercut detail that would have been impossible to mould and eject with regular hard plastic. The parts were also near indestructible, making them perfect playthings for younger modellers. Painting them was another

Fig 8.2 An Airfix 1:32 US Paratrooper, now moulded in K-resin, a harder type of plastic that is easier to paint.

matter and we'll come to that in a while!

In recent times manufacturers have switched to K-resin, a modified rubber polystyrene that, while retaining a certain amount of flexibility enabling ease of moulding and ejecting, is much harder and can be filed, filled and stuck together using normal model glue – more importantly paint adheres to the K-resin and stays there. While they may not be as flexible as they used to be in the physical sense, they are much more useful and modeller-friendly than before. Only the Airfix 1:76 figures continue to be moulded in polyethylene simply because the component design cannot accommodate K-resin moulding.

BLOWN VINYL

The late 1980s and early 1990s saw the arrival of large-scale figures moulded in 'blown' vinyl using a technique that allowed bigger, hollow shapes to be moulded in one piece. For the most part these kinds of kits were of science fiction, fantasy and horror subjects, produced by companies like Screamin', Horizon, Billiken and Max Factory. They required some careful cleanup and preparation, often involving heating the vinyl (either in hot water or with a hair dryer) so that it became soft and pliable, making it easier to remove parts from the pour stubs. Epoxy resin adhesives or superglues were required to fix the parts together. Although still produced today, being niche products aimed at experienced modellers, these kinds of kits tend to be on the expensive side and are not really recommended for beginners.

PAINTS

Regardless of what kind of medium a figure is moulded in, or indeed the subject matter, painting techniques are universal. It is perhaps no coincidence that modellers often refer to the 'art of figure painting' because, like its fine art counterpart, it often uses exactly the same paints and painting techniques used on canvas. There is, for example, a long tradition of using artists' oil paints, partly down to the fact that people were painting model solders before the advent of enamel model paints, but mainly because oils offer fine degrees of control and blending, in the same manner as fine art. Oil painting also offers the ability to mix any shade you want, especially when it comes to flesh tones, even with just a basic number of colours to hand. About the only downside is that oil paints can take a long time to dry, much longer than enamels or acrylics. Thus painting even a 1:35 figure can take days if not weeks.

The advent of quick-drying enamel paints brought figure painting more squarely into the modelling arena than fine art, and whole armies could be painted in hours. For the traditionalists, enamel paints meant that large areas (like uniforms) could be under-painted — again much like fine art — with the details being added using oils, thus speeding up the process immensely.

The rise in acrylic paints has seen some interesting shifts in both products and techniques with modellers. Even before the first commercially available acrylic paints for modellers (from Tamiya and Pactra) appeared, figure modellers were experimenting with tubes of artist's acrylics in much the same way as oils. The big advantage of acrylics were faster drying times, although they could be worked like oils by adding retardants to slow down the drying process, thus enabling blending of colours. About the only disadvantage with

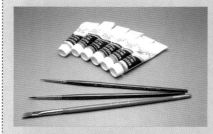

Fig 8.3 A basic selection of oil paints and brushes are all that is needed to get started on figure painting.

acrylics was psychological in as much as some modellers thought that water-based paints would not work on plastic!

One interesting innovation in recent years is the Panzer Aces range of acrylics by Vallejo in Spain and produced in conjunction with *Panzer Aces* magazine. It is more a complete painting system, consisting of a base tone (for example German Field Grey), and a lighter version for highlights. The range covers most of the popular uniform colours for German, British, American, Italian, Russian and Japanese uniforms of WWII, as well as more general colours like skin tones, wood, rust and mud. The availability of ready-mixed tonal variations does help take the guesswork out of shading.

EQUIPMENT

Figures can be painted with regular enamel or acrylic modelling paints, but for more advanced techniques, especially face painting, it is worth investing in a selection of oil paints. Small boxes of artists' oils can be found relatively cheaply these days and for the most part these are good quality, but for absolute consistency (in every sense) it is worth investing in some recognised brand names like Daler-Rowney, Windsor and Newton or Griffin Alkyds (the latter are faster drying). A basic selection of paints would be: white, black, red, yellow ochre, burnt sienna and ultramarine. From this almost any colour needed can be mixed, at least as far as basic face painting is concerned. Similarly, the same selection also serves for acrylics.

A small bottle of linseed oil is also worth considering – unlike white spirit or turpentine which thins and breaks down the pigments, linseed oil makes the paint more viscous but without affecting its covering power. There are also mediums that can be added to make the paint more gloss or matt. Similarly, there are retardants, flow enhancers and mediums available for acrylics that slow down the drying time, enabling them to be worked with like oils, or which alter their sheen.

One area the budding figure painter cannot neglect are paintbrushes. As noted in a previous chapter, the best results are usually achieved using quality paintbrushes and this especially applies to figure painting where absolute precision and control is required – a cheap brush that does not hold

Fig 8.4 Paint takes better to a clean, grease-free surface. A little dishwasher detergent and an old toothbrush are used to scrub this figure clean.

Fig 8.5 After rinsing and patting with a piece of tissue, the figure is left to dry.

its point or has stray hairs sticking out is a sure way of spoiling any attempts at painting. For scales between 1:76 and 1:35, a selection of round brushes from 000 up to a size 2 will suffice – for bigger scales it is worth considering a couple of medium flat brushes for covering larger areas. When it comes to choosing paints, mediums and brushes, a specialist art shop will be able to advise you on the best materials available.

Finally you'll need some mixing palettes – you can buy commercially available ones but anything from old jam jar lids and yoghurt pots to metal tea light containers can be utilised. One trick worth considering if using oil paints is to squeeze the colours out onto an old piece of cardboard first – this can help absorb the excess oil and take away any unwanted

sheen, before transferring over to the mixing palette.

PAINTING POLYETHYLENE FIGURES

As mentioned earlier, perhaps the first experiences many modellers will have of figures are the sets made by Airfix. The polyethylene plastic was often tricky to clean up and would burr and go 'fuzzy' if filed, paint would not stick and flake off, and most glues would not take, even superglue. Even 'hot' automotive paints like cellulose car sprays – which can attack and melt polystyrene if applied too heavily – would have little effect and just flake off when dry. The arrival of K-resin has largely solved these problems.

About the only way paint can be made to stick to polyethylene is to paint the

Fig 8.6 Careful blending of skin tones and subtle shading produces lifelike results.

Fig 8.7 Detail painting on the figure of The Doctor, even down to small highlights in the eyes and on the lips.

figures with a thin coat of PVA glue first — the PVA shrinks and clings to the polyethylene and provides the paint with a better surface to adhere to — it isn't foolproof, and the paint can still flake off with extensive handling, but it does offer some level of protection.

PREPARATION

Regardless of the moulding medium, the best way to ensure good results is to prepare the figure well prior to painting. Even a figure that appears clean may have some mould-release agent residue on it, or even grease picked up from the skin when handling. Add a drop of washing up liquid in some lukewarm water and use an old toothbrush to give the figure or figures a

good scrub. It can then be patted with a paper towel and left to dry.

A coat of primer provides a neutral base for subsequent colour coats. Matt white has long been favoured because not only does white add vibrancy to colours, especially yellows and reds that tend to be translucent (and both feature in skin tones), but matt white also absorbs some of the oil in oil paints and can help take the shine out of colours. Primer can be either brushed, painted or sprayed on in several thin coats and allowed to dry thoroughly.

FACES

For all the intricate painting that can feature on a figure model, almost the first thing any viewer will focus on is the face — it

is a natural reflex we carry over from interacting with people in the real world. It is also usually the thing a new modeller will neglect to address.

A figure model could have the most incredibly painted details on a uniform — say the tartan pattern on a Highlander — but if the face is poorly painted or overdone, then it spoils the whole effect. Conversely, a well-painted face can draw attention away from poorly painted uniform. So getting the face right is important, and to some extent techniques may need to be modified to suit different scales.

With 1:72 or 1:76 figures, detailed face painting is largely redundant and it is very easy to overdo things. A simple test is to view a person from the same distance as the figure you are painting and see how much detail you can actually see. This especially applies to the eyes — many figure models in smaller scales are spoiled by stark, wide-eyed expressions. Part of this is down to the fact that we record, and want to represent, details on models even if they may not actually be true to scale — as Chris Ellis once noted in *How To Go Plastic Modelling*, our impressions of the real thing don't necessarily scale down, so modellers try to paint eyes when, in truth, you'd never be able to see them when viewing a real person from an equivalent distance.

For painting faces we'll look at four techniques; the easy, intermediate, advanced and traditional approaches that range from good, quick results for the beginner to the more classical, fine art approach of using oils and blending techniques. In both we'll use a Caucasian face as an example.

THE EASY WAY

Whatever route you take for painting faces, the aim is to suggest shadows and highlights. Most modellers start with a base tone – this may not necessarily be the final flesh tone but just a foundation, akin to under-painting in fine art. For Caucasian skin this can vary from a pale pinkish tone to even a sandy yellow or brown depending on the effect you are after. Most model paint ranges these days have a decent flesh colour that should take out the guesswork of mixing, and most can be tweaked to personal preference.

For the really easy way, especially on small-scale figures in 1:76 or 1:72, paint the faces with the base tone flesh colour and allow to dry. Then mix up a thin wash of brown, either oils, enamels or acrylics, and apply this with a fine, pointed brush, allowing it to settle into the crevices and recessed detail on the face. Once happy with the result, allow this to dry thoroughly.

Now mix up a lighter shade of the base tone by adding a little white and drybrush this across the face using a slightly larger brush. The aim is to pick out the raised details and try and keep the effect subtle. The finished effect should be a hint of both

Fig 8.8 A member of the Airfix 1:24 Mosquito aircrew, slightly modified from the kit by adding the arm holding the map, and given a coat of white primer.

Fig 8.9 The flesh areas are picked out. On this figure acrylics were used as a base tone.

Fig 8.10 Burnt sienna oil paint was applied over the flesh areas, making sure all the recessed areas were covered.

Fig 8.11 After allowing the paint to settle for a few minutes, the excess is removed using a clean, dry brush.

shadows and highlights, adding a little more life to the face than a single coat of flesh coloured paint would achieve.

THE INTERMEDIATE APPROACH

This approach is slightly more involved, though still well within the means of the beginner. Start by under-painting the face

with a slightly darker tone than may be expected, perhaps by adding a few drops of brown to your flesh mix, and allow to dry.

Now take the unaltered base tone itself and gently drybrush the face – the aim is to gradually build up the base colour to cover the face, leaving the darker mix in any recessed areas, thus creating an impression

Fig 8.12 It may take several attempts, but the finished effect should leave paint in the recessed areas that softly blends into the base flesh tone.

Fig 8.13 Additional highlighting using a paler flesh mix, along with a touch of colour to the lips and cheeks, brings the figure to life. The eyes are touched in with a dark grey rather than black.

Fig 8.14 The uniform is painted, shaded and highlighted. The scarf is painted red with white polka-dots to add a touch of personality, before the model is given a finishing coat of matt varnish.

of shading. Again, leave to dry.

To pick up highlights, add a few drops of white to the base colour and again drybrush the face, but this time the touch should be light and the aim just to pick out sharp areas like the bridge of the nose, or maybe the brow and cheeks. Again, the finished effect should be an accentuation of light and shade rather than a stark depiction of it.

THE ADVANCED METHOD

Falling halfway between the simpler methods and the more traditional approach, this technique starts with a basic, unaltered flesh tone which is allowed to dry. Take some pure, un-thinned burnt sienna paint and apply over the whole face in a very thin coat. With the paint still wet, take a clean, flat brush and begin to work this over the face starting from the top down using the same motion as if drybrushing a paler tone. Give the brush a quick clean on a piece of rag or tissue after a few strokes (but do not rinse in thinner) and repeat the process. The aim is to start drawing the burnt sienna paint off the face, leaving traces of it in the recessed areas like the eyes, under the nose and chin. By keeping the brush dry,

the paint is gradually blended into the base tone creating a smooth effect.

After allowing this to dry thoroughly, a lighter mix of the flesh tone can be drybrushed over the face. The result should be a pleasing mix of soft shadows and a hint of highlights.

THE TRADITIONAL WAY

This is the more complicated method of working with oil paints or slow-drying acrylics to take advantage of the paint when 'wet', i.e. applying a flesh tone then blending in darker tones around. The choice here is to

Fig 8.15 The basic flesh mix has been applied using oil paints, using the slow drying time to blend in shadows and highlights.

Fig 8.16 More shading and blending, as well as painting the eye sockets using a pinkish/white.

Fig 8.17 The life jacket is given a first coat of paint – yellow is a translucent colour so it needs several coats to become more opaque.

mix up a custom flesh colour and either apply direct to a white undercoat or a base tone as mentioned previously. Either way, start out by taking some white paint and adding a hint of yellow ochre, using a suitable thinning medium like linseed oil. The paint should be creamy both in terms of appearance and consistency – an off-white with just a hint of yellow. Now add a tiny amount of red – be aware that you'll actually need less than you may think as even the smallest amount can turn things too vivid and pink. It may take some experimentation to get the right shade – this is quite normal!

With the required shade achieved, take a pointed brush like a number 0 and apply the paint to the face, adding a little at a time and working this onto the surface until the face is evenly covered. The beauty of oils is that time is on your side so there is no need to rush or apply heavy coats, and any brush marks or ridges can be smoothed out with a dry, clean brush.

The next step is to start adding shadows which can be worked into the wet paint. Take a small amount of burnt sienna and add to the basic flesh tone mix – aim for a slightly darker look and using a fine pointed brush apply this to areas like the

furrows either side of the nose, under the eyebrows, nose and lower lip, around the ears and along the hairline. Again use less than you think you need and concentrate on adding the colour rather than blending at this stage.

With the shading completed, it can now be blended using a clean, dry brush by working on a small area at a time, gently drawing the darker areas into the base tone. Actual blending techniques come down to personal preference and experience, and there is no substitute for practise to find out which method works best. The aim is to achieve a subtle graduation between the darker and lighter tones, subtly emphasizing the shadows rather than exaggerating them.

Once you are happy with the shading you can start adding the highlights. This can be done either by adding white to the base tone mix, or applying white direct to the face and blending it in. Areas to aim for are the bridge of the nose, chin, cheekbones and ears. Again, use less paint than you think and blend using a clean, dry brush. Keep checking your work and see if you are achieving the effect you are after – again, it all comes down to practise and the great thing about oils is that if you are not happy with your work, you can remove the wet paint with a cotton swab, pat dry and start again. The same shading and highlighting techniques can be used for hands and other areas of flesh, for example shirtless gun crews.

With the basic flesh tones applied, it is now time to add a little colour – and the emphasis is on little – by mixing a small amount of red into the base tone and applying this to the cheeks. As mentioned previously, it only takes a minute amount of red to tint a colour, and it can be a fine line between enough and too much. The aim is to suggest a hint of colour in the cheeks rather than end up with something looking like a pantomime dame! The same mix can be added to the lips, adding a touch more white to the lower lip for contrast.

EYES

As mentioned earlier, if a face makes or breaks a figure, it is usually the eyes that tip the balance. There is something to be said for the argument that painting eyes even in 1:35 is also redundant, for the same reasons already outlined for smaller scales – the likelihood of being able to pick out details when viewing a real person from the equivalent distance as a scale model figure is slim.

Certainly when modelling figures from harsh environments like the desert or jungle, faces would tend to be squinting against the bright sunlight so modellers would be fully justified is adding no eye detail at all – a model of a wide-eyed Afrika Korps soldier from the Western Desert would look a little incongruous!

In scales larger than 1:35 face painting becomes more complex in terms of the amount of detail painting, but easier in terms of physical size. Kits like the 1:12 Airfix figures, or the 1:9 models in the Doctor Who 'Welcome Aboard' set benefit from not only painting eyes, but also details such as the iris and even highlights.

Perhaps the biggest, though understandable, mistake when painting eyes is to make the whites pure white, and the iris and pupil detail black – the result can often be too stark, bordering on the unnerving, looking more like a shop mannequin or something from a Mardi Gras parade.

The first step is working out how much white would be visible for the scale and subject. If adding eye whites, use a very pale grey or mix the smallest amount of red or brown into the white, just enough to take the starkness away. On larger scale figures a wash of thinned red can be added to suggest the veins at the corners, which also adds a little more depth and character.

In scales like 1:35 the iris and pupils can be treated as one, but rather than using black, mix an off-grey perhaps with a touch of blue to take the edge from the opacity. Applying iris/pupil detail requires a fine brush, a steady hand and just the right amount of paint. It is very easy to end up with figures that are boss-eyed, looking in opposite directions or with eyes rolling upwards like zombies – fine for zombies, but perhaps not for a Battle of Britain pilot! One trick favoured by some modellers is to paint the eye socket a dark grey colour then touch the edges in with an off-white. To some extent this does offer a little more control because it allows the effect of the centre of the eye to be built up gradually.

In larger scales separate pupil and iris detail can be added, and subtleties in actual eye colour added, either pale or dark, but with the iris added using a dark grey rather than black – again the aim should be use subdued colours that look natural rather than something too stark and comical. A thin dark line to suggest eyelashes can also be added above the eye. As a finishing touch a small white highlight can also be added and perhaps even a touch of gloss varnish to add a little shine.

HAIR

Many modellers rarely paint a head of hair on figures simply because they are often sculpted wearing headgear of sorts, either hats, caps or helmets. But some figures do come bareheaded, the old 1:32 Airfix Multipose sets for one and some of the recent 1:35 Tamiya and Dragon figures. Additionally some white metal and resin kits feature bearded figures – either way they all share the same techniques.

Again, you need to start with a base colour and this all depends on the hair colour you wish to depict. For black hair it may better to start off with a very dark grey and use pure black for shading, adding a hint of pale blue to the base colour for highlighting. Try to keep this on the subtle side so as not to create the impression of greying hair, unless of course that is the effect you are after.

Dark earth is a good starting point for brown hair, adding burnt sienna for shadows and a hint of yellow for highlights. Dark earth itself can also be darkened or lightened as a base tone for different variations, or even with red added for a more chestnut effect.

For blonde hair, start with a base coat of sand and add white to create highlights – the paler the hair colour, the more delicate any shading needs to be, so add small amounts of burnt sienna to the base colour to create a subtle darkening. The same applies to grey or silver hair where shading

Fig 8.18 The hair is added and the uniform is painted RAF blue/grey . Further shading and highlighting will reduce the toy-like finish.

Fig 8.19 Areas around the pockets and seams are lined in a darker shade of the base colour, while a lighter mix picks out the highlights on edges and corners.

and highlighting is achieved through the very slightest changes in tone.

For shaved heads or stubble on beards, mix a little brown or grey into the flesh mix and apply small quantities at a time, blending into the skin tone to build up a 'five o'clock shadow' effect. Finally the eyebrows need adding, again using toned-down colours to just suggest a hint of hair rather than overdoing it with stark lines, which will give you a figure that looks like Groucho Marx!

CLOTHING

Pretty much the same painting techniques used for faces also apply when it comes to painting uniforms, costumes and clothing. While some modellers will custom mix clothing colours using oils, working the paint when wet much like face painting, many prefer to apply a base tone using off-the-shelf enamels or acrylics and supplement these with shading and highlighting techniques.

Taking an RAF pilot's uniform as an example, the jacket and trousers are given a

Fig 8.20 The hair is carefully picked out using lighter and darker streaks, painted in the direction of hair growth starting at the crown outwards.

Fig 8.21 With the final few details added and a coat of matt varnish, this 1:24 Mosquito pilot is finished.

basic coat of Humbrol 96 RAF blue/grey enamels and allowed to dry. Using oil paints, some black is added to the base colour with a touch of linseed oil to blend it all together and this is used to line the pockets, lapels and placket. Use a clean brush to blend the darker colour into the base tone. This same approach can be used to accentuate folds in the clothing, though for the most part these tend to be well moulded enough to form their own natural shadows.

When it comes to highlighting, the same classic techniques can be used by adding white to the base colour and blending this in, though a much faster method is to gently drybrush using the same paler tone to pick up the edges and folds – if choosing the latter, make sure the shaded areas are thoroughly dry first.

The lifejacket is painted with several thin coats of yellow to build up the colour. For shading, add small amounts of burnt sienna to the yellow to produce a darker, richer shade – black tends to make yellow go muddy.

For boots and footwear, under-paint with either very dark grey or dark brown enamels or acrylics, then shade with black

oil paint, blending away the excess. For well-worn or cracked leather you can drybrush variations of glossy blacks or browns over the matt base colour, building up the layers with increasingly lighter tones.

EQUIPMENT

It is easy to treat equipment on a figure as a bit of an afterthought, but using the same shading techniques can enhance these items considerably. For the wooden butts on rifles and machine guns, paint them matt dark brown and shade with black at the edges. The centre of the butt can be highlighted with a lighter brown and blended so there is a shift of tone. For the metal parts there are several approaches, perhaps the most effective is to paint the metal parts matt black and then drybrush with gunmetal. Some modellers prefer to custom mix their own gunmetal with black and silver, adding a drop of dark blue to impart the look of the chemical protective 'bluing' process applied to metals on guns, and then shading with black.

The metal blades on spades and shovels use pretty much the same approach, making sure to keep the cutting edge a brighter silver. For unsheathed swords or daggers, a brighter metal effect can be achieved by applying an undercoat of gloss black then using buffable metallic paints like Humbrol Metalcote. On cast white metal figures it is easier to polish up the actual metal with the side of a pin or sewing

Fig 8.22 The finished Mosquito aircrew painted using slightly different approaches.

drybrush this on to pick up the details. It can take some practise to get a feel for just the right amount of lightening and drybrushing needed, and if your figure ends up looking frosty or 'sugar coated' then it is probably overdone and you need to take everything back a bit. Washes of a darker colour can also be used to add depth, but again subtlety is the watchword. The beauty of multi-figure sets is that there are plenty of figures to practise on.

FINISHING TOUCHES

Even if only modelling a single figure without any scenic context, small details can tell a story. A WWI soldier with glossy muddy boots and puttees will suggest the horror and misery of the Somme. Darker patches across the back, chest and under the arms of a Australian soldier will impart the sweltering heat of the jungle. Paler and redder skin tones on an Eighth Army or Afrika Korps figure hints at tanlines and sunburn in the harsh desert. Even a small amount of red dust on a US Marine from the 1960s or early 1970s will instantly place him in the clay soils of Vietnam.

Like any other model, figures also benefit from a final varnish coat, either to impart the correct final sheen, or to protect the finish from handling. Water-based varnishes tend to work best as they are non-yellowing and there is less risk of them lifting or reacting with paint, though it goes without question to make sure all colour

Fig 8.23 As figure-painting skills improve you may wish to tackle more complex camouflage patterns, as seen on this Airfix 1:32 British paratrooper. Note also his intricate helmet webbing. Model by Adam Cooper.

coats are totally dry, especially if using oils. These can be brushed on using a medium, flat brush, taking care that the varnish doesn't pool into folds and crevices.

PAINT, PRACTISE AND PERFECT

Again, there is no substitute for practise and the more you try out various techniques and approaches, finding out which ones work and which ones don't, the more you'll learn and perfect your own methods, whether it be painting figures as an addition to an aircraft or tank model, or as an interest in itself.

needle, then coating with gloss varnish to stop the metal oxidising.

SMALLER SCALES

Just like painting faces in smaller scales, clothing and uniforms do not require the same level of shading and highlighting in 1:72 or 1:76 as in 1:35 since, due to the small size, it is very easy to overdo the effects and make the figures look a little comic.

The simplest way of adding some life to small scale figures is to apply a base colour, for example the field grey on a German soldier, allow to dry, then mix up a lighter version by adding white and lightly

1:12 Yeoman of the Guard

1:12 AIRFIX YEOMAN OF THE GUARD

Airfix first introduced scale model figures in 1959 with a series of 1:12 kits that included a Lifeguard Trumpeter, Coldstream Guardsman and the Yeoman of the Guard and went on to include British monarchs like King Henry VIII and Queen Elizbath, as well as historical figures like Oliver Cromwell, Napoleon Bonaparte and Joan of Arc.

In later years Airfix introduced a 1:12 French Grenadier of the Imperial Guard, a mounted Bengal Lancer and a 'Showjumper' that bore a striking resemblance to HRH Princess Anne. Perhaps the rarest of all the 1:12 figures is the Boy Scout, which commands a very high price on the second-hand market even though it had a six year production run from 1965 to 1971.

In more recent years Airfix returned to large scale figures in the form of 1:9 England footballers from the (then) current side in 2004. These had limited appeal and can be found on auction sites relatively cheaply — could these be the rare collectable items of the future?

The subject of this build is the Yeoman of the Guard. It first had a long production run of 18 years until 1977 then after a rest in 1978 it came back out for 1979 only. Since then it has not been in the Airfix catalogue but the Yeoman, along with the Lifeguard Trumpeter and Coldstream Guardsman, are due to be released together in a 'London Figures' set in conjunction with the 2012 London Olympic Games.

CONSTRUCTION

The Yeoman figure comprises 62 parts but 22 of these are the ribbons that encircle his hat. **See Fig 1.1**. Construction begins with the body, which is a case of simply cementing the front and back together. Next to construct are the five parts that make up the lower tunic. It can be fiddly to try and glue the four skirts to the base plate at the same time as it's quite important to get the joins together correctly. Begin by gluing two of the rear skirts together and then glue to the base plate. Before the glue has set you can gently move

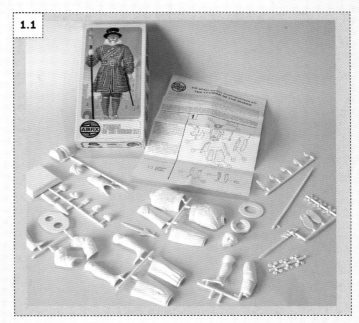

1.1

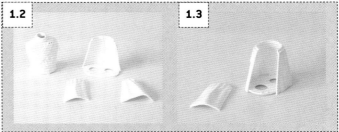

1.2   **1.3**

the parts until you are happy with the final position. **See Fig 1.2**.

The third and fourth skirts can be added and again gently slide the parts as the glue is setting to make nice tight joins. Now leave all of these parts to dry thoroughly. **See Fig 1.3 and Fig 1.4**.

Once the cement has set, glue the body upper and lower parts together. They only fit one way but you will need to ensure that the edges of the shoulder belt line up on the rear of the figure. **See Fig 1.5**.

The head, arms, hands and legs are also made up of two halves. They all have a seam that will need sanding and a small amount of filler will be needed to finish off. After light sanding the joins should be hardly noticeable. The Yeoman's left leg (shown on the right in the picture) has had the seam filled and sanded, the one on the left hasn't. **See Fig 1.6**.

The hat was also assembled at this stage and the body parts were set aside to dry. **See Fig 1.7**.

Locate and cement the arms to the body. Once dry a little filler is applied to the join between the shoulders and the tops of the arms and sanded down. Locate the legs into the two large holes under the body and position the legs so the toes are pointing slightly outwards. Once the glue has set add the soles to the shoes and leave for a while. After checking to see if any of the build so far requires any filler you can now cement the figure to the base. There is a flap on the left shoulder blade that keeps the shoulder belt in place; don't forget to add it!

Once the glue has set the model can be primed – because the finished figure will be painted red, it is best to use a white undercoat or primer as red tends to be a translucent colour, and a grey base would make the red appear slightly darker. White automotive primer is used on this model. The hands are not fitted at this stage as it is easier to paint the detail on the figure without them. **See Figs 1.8 and 1.9**.

PAINTING THE FACE AND HEAD

The head is moulded in two halves comprising of the face and the rear of the head. The seam runs down behind the ears and into the jaw line. Scrape away the seam with a scalpel blade and fill if necessary to ensure a smooth join. To make painting easier, the head is mounted onto a wooden skewer and held in place with a blob of Blu-Tack.

The face is painted using various Vallejo acrylics that come in a

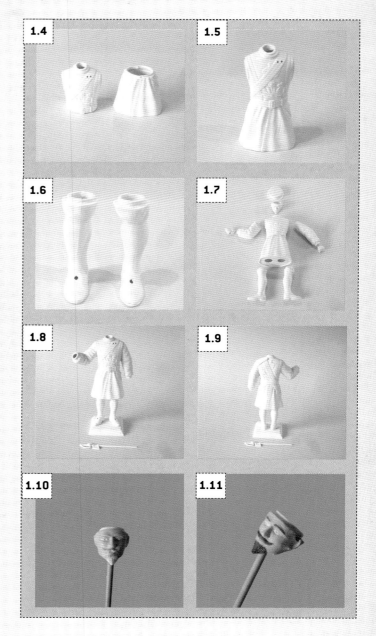

set of face and flesh colours. You can use Humbrol paints but their Flesh colour (H61) is a little too yellow. If using Humbrol enamels use H61 with other light tan and sand colours mixed together to obtain the various shades and lighten with white or darken with a little brown — don't use black, it's too dark and can turn the flesh colours a dirty muddy grey colour. Vallejo's Basic Flesh Tone is used all over the face and neck going into the hairline. **See Fig 1.10.**

The whites of the eyes are painted with white toned down with the tiniest amount of flesh colour to make the white less stark — the whites of your eyes are never 'brilliant white'. The hair, eyebrows, moustache and beard are a simple mix of black and white to make a medium grey. **See Fig 1.11.**

Vallejo's Burnt Umber, slightly lightened, is painted on the darker areas of the face, under the eyes, in and around the ears, furrows of forehead and around the nose and mouth. The eyes are picked out in a light blue/grey colour using black, white and a touch of Prussian blue. **See Fig 1.12.**

Blending Vallejo's Light Flesh Tone, Dark Flesh Tone and white brings out the contours of the face. Make the front of the nose, cheekbones and areas of the forehead lighter and the jaw line, neck and lower face slightly darker. It takes a little practise and you may find you need to keep going over the face a few times with the different paints to bring the face to life. The pupils of the eyes are dotted with black and the tiniest highlight with a speck of white in each eye just to give them a glint. **See Fig 1.13.**

The Yeoman's hair is painted grey a few times making each coat lighter and then finishing with some white paint. All there is left to do is paint in his nostrils and use a little rose colour for his lips. **See Figs 1.14 and 1.15.**

PAINTING THE PARTISAN (HALBERD)

The Yeoman of the Guard carries two weapons: the eight foot long Partisan and a sword that hangs off the shoulder belt. The blade of the Partisan is polished steel with black and gold decoration. The bottom end of the Partisan is fitted with a steel sleeve that protects

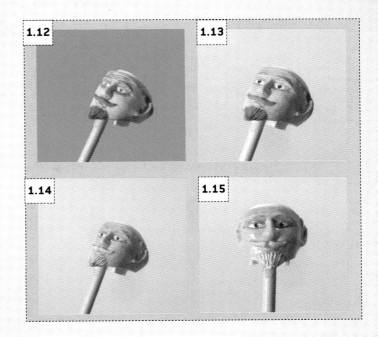

the end of the wooden pole. Polished Aluminium from the Humbrol Metal Cote range is used and buffed to a bright finish. The details are applied using two coats of Vallejo black. The gold detail on the Partisan is painted with a very steady hand using a very fine brush! **See Fig 1.16.**

PAINTING THE UNIFORM

The uniform was painted using Humbrol Insignia Red H174 which is about the closest match in the Humbrol range. Let the figure dry thoroughly for about four days for the paint to harden off completely. **See Fig 1.17.**

The majority of the tunic's decorations are black stripes edged in gold. As the gold edging is narrower than the black it is easier to paint that first and then infill with the black afterwards. When painting the gold be careful not to get it on the red areas but don't worry too much if some gets on to the black areas as this will be covered later. Once

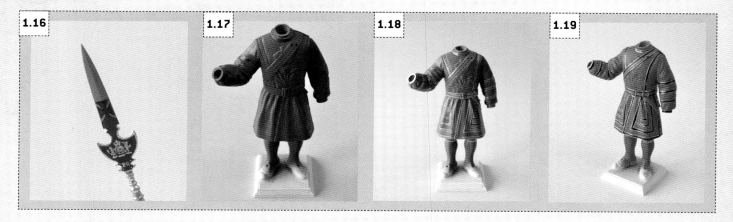

the gold is done fill in-between with black paint, then leave the figure to dry completely. **See Fig 1.18 and Fig 1.19**.

The embroidered decoration on the tunic comprises of a crown, a thistle, rose and shamrock under which is a foliage pattern underlined with a scroll. There are also the 'E' and 'R' motifs. Begin by painting the Crown and the rose a deep red colour and paint the thistle, shamrock and foliage black as that is the colour of their outline. **See Fig 1.20**.

Gold paint is used for the details on the crown and the centre of the rose. Using a fine brush paint the outline and detail on the foliage and also add a few flecks to the bottom of the thistle. Finally gold is used to infill the 'E' and 'R' leaving a black outline. These letters on the real tunic are slightly darker than the rest of the gold and this is replicated with some antique gold paint. The shamrock, five stripes on the rose and the top of the thistle are a light green and the thistle is finished off with a few light strokes of pale blue – this is only for the thistle on the rear of the uniform as the shoulder belt covers the front one.

The scroll pattern just above the belt line is yellow edged in gold with a little black to represent the words 'DIEU' and 'DROIT'. The scroll centre is not visible on this model but for interest it reads 'ET MON' (i.e. 'God and my Right' – the motto of the British Monarch). The last

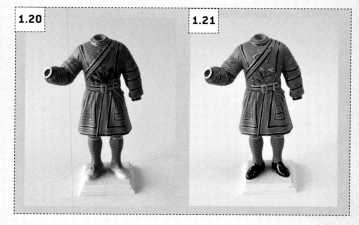

parts to paint in this section are the shoes; these are gloss black with matt black soles. **See Fig 1.21**.

PAINTING AND ADDING THE SMALL DETAILS

Before adding the ribbons for the hat paint four red, the next four white and the last ones blue. Although there are 24 ribbons to the hat only 17 actually fit! They should be applied in the red, white, blue order. The sword is painted black with a gold handle and gold bottom end. The rosettes that fit to the shoes and knee are also a mixture of red, white

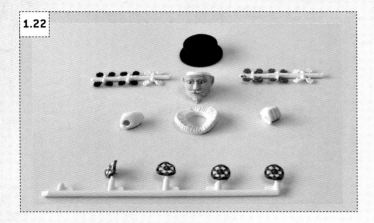

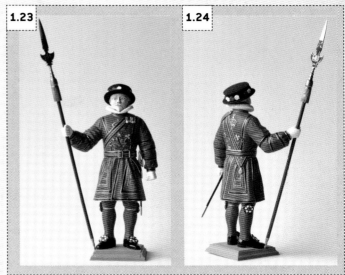

and blue. The gloves and ruff are painted white with a little light grey shading. The hat is painted matt black. **See Fig 1.22**.

The final details can now be cemented to the body starting with the ruff, head and hat – the latter will fit either way round. The gloved hands are added ensuring the hole in the right hand lines up to the edge of the right shoe ready for the Partisan to be slotted in once the cement on the hand has dried.

The sword is glued in place. There is a length of the shoulder belt with the sword piece and this should be painted to match the rest of the shoulder belt. The rosettes are fixed to the knees and shoes. The base of the model can be painted a mid-stone colour. This leaves just one more piece; the medals.

One of the criteria to become a Yeoman is that you need to have earned certain medals. Two of these have to be the Long Service and Good Conduct medal (LSGC), and at least one campaign medal. Other medals that can be included are Jubilee medals and decorations such as DSOs, MBEs and OBEs. There is a position order for these reflecting their importance. The medal nearest the left arm would almost certainly be the LSGC then moving to the right (as worn) they would then be Jubilee medals if earned, next are campaign medals and then finally decorations. This Yeoman was decorated with:

- LSGC (maroon with grey edging, silver medallion);
- Silver Jubilee medal (mainly blue with white and red, silver medallion);
- Golden Jubilee medal (mainly white with blue and red, gold medallion);
- Northern Ireland campaign medal (purple with green edging, silver medallion); and
- MBE (red with grey edging and centre stripe, silver cross).

With the medals painted the figure is now finished! **See Figs 1.23 and 1.24**.

Acknowledgement: Personal thanks go to Yeoman Messenger Sergeant Major Clive Stevens and Yeoman William Norton for their invitation to St James' Palace, London to see first hand the Yeoman of the Guard uniform and to take reference photographs for this model build. For further information see www.yeomenoftheguard.com.

Step by step build 6 by Adam Cooper

1:76 Diorama

1:76 AIRFIX DIORAMA

2010 saw the release by Airfix of a new range of ruined buildings aimed at the diorama builder and wargamer. The first two releases were the European Ruined Workshop (A75001) and a European Ruined Café (A75002).

Produced in resin, these come ready built with separate photo etched window frames and clear plastic sheet for glazing. These just require painting of the finely detailed surfaces either using the suggested paint schemes illustrated on the boxes or using the modeller's own choice of colours.

The aim of this build is not a blow-by-blow account of painting the buildings themselves but to describe some of the simple techniques to make a small inexpensive diorama base for use as a scenic display of not just the buildings themselves but any suitable vehicles and figures the modeller decides to place upon it.

For this project an inexpensive cork message board slightly smaller than A3 is used as it comes with a frame and is sturdy enough to build the diorama straight on to it. It is always best to plan out your diorama and the kinds of features and details you wish to portray, as well as the composition of the scene. With this diorama the intention is to have a pan-European cobbled road junction at which the two Airfix buildings can be placed, the café building being on a paved stretch of road and the workshop being situated within a small yard surrounded by a high concrete faced wall. The cobbled road provides enough space for several vehicles to be displayed as desired, while the layout also allows viewing from different directions. **See Fig 1.1.**

The materials used in this build are:
• Millet seeds
• 4mm thick art board
• Quick drying ready mixed filler
• Thick card

1.1

• Thin cardboard
• 4mm square section balsa wood
• PVA wood glue
• Johnsons Klear acrylic floor polish
• Hornby Scenic scatter grass and tufts

The 'kerb' stones are chopped up from 4mm square section Balsa wood and glued to the base forming the edges of the paved areas. 4mm art board strips are laid down as 'foundations' for the walling to be added later. **See Fig 1.2 and Fig 1.3.**

Rather than replicate a tarmac road, this diorama aims to depict a more European cobbled street. Experimentation with various materials can yield surprising results – in this instance dried millet seeds, readily available in the health food section of supermarkets – are used for the cobbles, these being just the right size. The millet is spread across the road area in a single layer working from one end to the other. Slight tapping of the base enables the seeds to 'settle' next to each other in a fairly tight pattern. Once the layer has been spread be careful not to nudge the base and dislodge any cobbles. The only way to fix the 'cobbles' down is to use a liquid glue of some sort – either thinned PVA, a thinned paint or varnish etc – applied onto the cobbles so that it flows amongst them and glues them down as it dries. Unfortunately the millet absorbs moisture from any liquid it is in contact with, causing it to swell ever so slightly. This isn't immediately noticeable but across the width of our road this expansion will cause an unsightly buckling of the surface that will require removal and then relaying of the millet cobbles and applying glue again.

The millet is fixed in place using a mix of PVA glue and Johnson's Klear Floor Polish, with some acrylic paint added to colour the mixture, acting as a guide to where it has been applied. When completely covered it is best to put this somewhere warm and flat to speed up the drying process and hopefully cut down the amount of expansion caused by liquid being absorbed. After about an hour take a look at it, and if any lumps are developing scrape them off to leave some gaps. When fully dried highlight these gaps with a pen and then refill with millet and re-apply the glue to that area and put aside to dry again. **See Fig 1.4**.

With the basic cobbled surface laid, the gaps in-between can now be 'grouted' using a ready mixed tube of wall filler, applied to a small area at a time and spread thinly with a palette knife using fingers wrapped in a plastic bag for protection. After leaving to dry any air holes can be quickly filled – the result should be a more even, cobbled road surface. **See Fig 1.5**.

Painting can now be carried out either by brush or airbrush. A base coat of Sea Grey H27 is ideal, but any darkish grey will do. **See Fig 1.6**.

Dry brushing with a slightly lighter grey, in this case Steel Grey H87, is applied across the road surface. **See Fig 1.7**.

A couple of dark grey washes are applied all over to accentuate the recessed detail. **See Fig 1.8**.

Finally a light dry brushing of satin varnish gives the cobbles a very slight, worn sheen as seen on the real thing.

WALLING

Strips of 4mm art board are cut to the desired scale height – in this case 8ft – and then a thin coating of quick drying filler is spread across both the main surfaces. Unless aiming for a pristine finish any lumps, bumps and spreading marks will add to the character of the finished wall. **See Fig 1.9**.

After the filler has dried the surface can be distressed, digging and scraping away the surface filler, carving cracks with a pin as well as digging into the foam core of the art board for more serious damage. The metal ferrule of an old paintbrush can be used as a cutter on the expanded foam interior of the art board, giving the impression of stones used in the wall's construction. Use of liquid poly, which dissolves expanded polystyrene, can also be used to great effect. **See Fig 1.10**.

After damaging the walls as required they can be painted Light Grey H64 and Ochre H83. **See Fig 1.11**.

The surface is drybrushed in lighter shades of the wall's base colour in this case, Camouflage Grey H28 and Light Grey H147. This shows off the rough surface of the filler to great effect. **See Fig 1.12**.

A wash of heavily thinned dark grey and dark brown paint is now applied to enhance the shadow areas. **See Fig 1.13**.

The walls can be finished off with capping slates from painted card or even curved clay tiles recreated by cutting a suitably thick drinking straw in half lengthwise. After slicing tiles from these half round strips and gluing them to the top of the wall they can be painted a terracotta colour.

GROUNDWORK

The groundwork for this base is created in two ways. The first is to use layered polystyrene sheeting that are cut and shaped as needed with any gaps filled. **See Fig 1.14**.

The second was to build up features using card formers and layering glue soaked paper (in true papier maché form) across these to form the shape required. **See Fig 1.15**.

For either of these methods, a PVA Glue mix is liberally spread

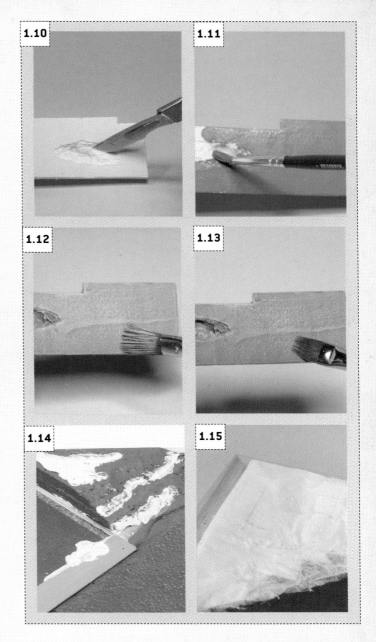

over the area to be covered with scatter material – this area could have been pre-painted a suitable colour or the glue can be appropriately coloured with acrylic paint, watercolours, even food colouring. **See Fig 1.16**.

The scenic scatter materials are spread over the glue; a slight pressing down can help with adhesion. Missing patches can be re-covered with more glue and scatter material. **See Fig 1.17**.

After drying the base needs to be shaken over a tray or bin liner to catch the loose unglued scatter material. This can be re-used if need be. If several different scatter materials are required a good idea is to glue them down individually; that way the excess material won't get mixed up.

Trees and bushes or other permanent features can be glued down with PVA glue. **See Fig 1.18**.

HARDSTANDINGS

Pavements and hardstandings, unless intended as seriously bumpy, can be portrayed with any flat card type material, painted suitable colours. Paving slabs can be marked out with a thin indelible ink pen or thin tipped drafting isograph pen. **See Fig 1.19**.

LITTLE EXTRAS

Rubble can be easily made from plaster filler coloured with water colours or crushed stone cat litter which is a very good rock material that comes in a very pale stone colour. However this can be easily re-coloured using paint, some thinner, mixing it all together and then allowing it to dry – the thinner stops the paint 'gluing' all the bits together. This rubble material can then be scattered or glued down as required. Additional items such as fencing and street furniture can be scratch built or sourced from the Hornby railway scenic range as well as other wargames or model manufacturers.**See Figs 1.20–1.24**.

1.16

1.17

1.18

1.19

RESOURCES

The growth of the internet has lead to huge number of resources now available for the modeller – so many that you could easily fill a book with them!

This listing, by no means exhaustive or comprehensive, includes some of the major manufacturers, organisations, publishers and forums.

In terms of resources, perhaps the best single site is Tony Matteliano's Scale Model Index, which lists hundreds of websites.

http://www.scalemodelindex.com

MANUFACTURERS

Airfix	www.airfix.com
Humbrol	www.humbrol.com
Revell	www.revell.com (North America)
	www.revell.de/en (Germany)
Tamiya	www.tamiya.com /english/e-home.htm (Japanese site in English)
	www.tamiyausa.com (Tamiya America)
Italeri	www.italeri.com
Trumpeter	www.trumpeter-china.com
Hobby Boss	www.hobbyboss.com
Hasegawa	www.hasegawa-model.co.jp
Dragon	www.dragon-models.com
Academy	www.academy.co.kr
Minicraft	www.minicraft models.com
AMT/Polar Lights/MPC	www.round2models.com
Moebius	www.moebiusmodels.com
MPM	www.mpmshop.cz
Eduard	www.eduard.cz
Xtradecal/Xtracolor/Xtracrylix	www.hannants.co.uk
Model Alliance	www.theaviation workshop.co.uk

WEBSITES

Britmodeller	www.britmodeler.com
Hyperscale	www.hyperscale.com
Aircraft Resource Center	www.aircraftresource center.com
Airfix Tribute Forum	http://airfixtributeforum. myfastforum.org
Airfix Collecting Forum	http://airfixcollecting. forumup.be/
Aussie Modeller International	www.aussiemodeller.com

Internet Modeler
www.internetmodeler.com
Modelling Madness
modelingmadness.com
Steel Navy
www.steelnavy.com

MAGAZINES AND BOOKS

Airfix Model World
www.airfixmodelworld.com
Scale Aircraft Modelling
Military Modelcraft International
Toy Soldier Collector
www.guidelinepublications.co.uk
Scale Aviation Modeller
Military Aircraft Monthly
Scale Military Modeller
http://sampublications.com
Military In Scale
http://www.traplet.com/
Tamiya Magazine International
Model Military International
Model Airplane International
http://www.adhpublishing.com
Fine Scale Modeler
http://www.finescale.com
Military Modelling
www.militarymodelling.com
http://www.ospreypublishing.com/
Squadron Signal
www.squadronsignalpublications.com

Ian Allan Publishing
www.ianallanpublishing.com
Conway Maritime Press
www.conwaypublishing.com

ORGANISATIONS

IPMS (UK) www.ipms-uk.co.uk
IPMS (USA) www.ipmsusa.org
British Model Soldier Society
www.btinternet.com/ffmodel.soldiers
The Armour Modelling and Preservation
Society
www.ampsarmor.org/ampssite/links.aspx
MAFVA (Miniature Armoured Fighting Vehicle
Association)
www.mafva.net
Perth Military Modelling Site
www.perthmilitarymodelling.com

BIBLIOGRAPHY

How to go Plastic Modelling, Chris Ellis,
Patrick Stephens Limited, 1968
How to Make Model Aircraft, Chris Ellis,
Hamlyn, 1974
Scale Model Aircraft in Plastic Card, Harry
Woodman, Model & Allied Publications,
1975
Making Model Aircraft, Bryan Philpott,
Patrick Stephens Limited, 1976
Aircraft of the Royal Air Force Since 1918,
Owen Thetford, Putnam Aeronautical, 1979
Scale Models in Plastic, Roger Chesneau,
Conway Maritime Press, 1979
Jane's Encyclopedia of Aviation, Jane's
Publishing Company Limited, 1980
*Military Models and Dioramas: The Verlinden
Way. Volume III, On Plastic Wings*, Francois
Verlinden, Verlinden Publications, 1983
(various editions)
*How To Build Plastic Aircraft Models - A
Complete How-To-Do-It Guide to Basic And
Advanced Modeling Techniques*, Roscoe
Creed, Kalmbach Publishing Company,
1985
Detailing Scale Model Aircraft, Mike Ashey,
Kalmbach Publishing Company, 1994
Brassey's Master Class: Master Modellers,
Robin Smith, Brassey's (UK) Ltd., 1997
*Airfix: Celebrating 50 Years of the Greatest
Plastic Kits in the World*, Arthur Ward,
Harper Collins, 1999
*Celebration of Flight: The Aviation Art of Roy
Cross*, Arthur Ward and Roy Cross, Crowood
Press, 2002
Military Vehicle Modelling, Phil Greenwood,
Crowood Press, 2002
Scale Aircraft Modelling, Mark Stanton,
Crowood Press, 2002
*F.A.Q.: Frequently Asked Questions on AFV
Painting Techniques (Modelling Manuals)*,
Miguel Jimenez, Andrea Press, 2005
Armour Modelling, John Prigent, Osprey
Publishing, 2006
*F.A.Q.: Frequently Asked Questions about
Techniques Used for Constructing &
Painting Aircraft*, J. M. Villalba, Andrea
Press, 2009
The Vintage Years of Airfix Box Art, Roy
Cross, Crowood Press, 2009
The Boys' Book of Airfix, Arthur Ward, Ebury
Press, 2009
*James May's Toy Stories: The Airfix
Handbook*, James May, Conway, 2010
Airfix Kits, Trevor Pask, Shire, 2010
Aircraft Modelling, Brett Green, Osprey
Publishing, 2010

GLOSSARY

Aftermarket parts General term referring to products that supplement boxed model kits, intended to update, super-detail, or modify the kit. These may be alternative decals or detail sets in photo-etched metal or cast resin.

AFV Acronym; Armoured Fighting Vehicles, e.g. tanks, armoured cars, or armoured personnel carriers.

Ailerons Moving control surfaces of an aircraft's wings.

Aircrew Generic term for flight crew of an aircraft, including pilot, navigator/observer, gunner, bombardier etc.

Airscrew Propeller assembly of an aircraft.

Amphibian Aircraft or vehicle which can operate on land or water.

Anhedral Angle of 'droop' of an aircraft's wing from root to tip.

Applique armour Armour plates added, often crudely, to the hull of a tank.

Barbette Protective circular armoured housing around a warship's gun, or alternatively the non-rotating drum beneath a gun turret that protects shell/ammunition hoist etc. In an aircraft the term refers to a gun mounting with a restricted arc of fire, e.g. a tail gun.

Bogie Assembly that carries a tank's road wheels, or a pivoted frame carrying a train's wheels.

Bow The front of a ship.

Box art Artwork commissioned by kit companies to illustrate the packaging of a model kit.

Bridge Main element of a ship's superstructure, from where it is navigated and commanded. Also known as conning tower, esp. in the context of submarines.

Canard Smaller forward surface in front of an aircraft's main wing.

Canopy Transparent cockpit cover of an aircraft.

Chord Width of an aircraft's tail surface, wing etc.

Conversion Custom variant of a standard model kit, achieved through scratch-building parts, combining two or more kits, or adding aftermarket accessories etc.

Counter-stern Overhanging stern of a ship.

Cupola Rotating hatch atop tank turret, for commander's use in action.

Davits Fittings on ship's side to hoist and hold boats, or occasionally anchors or torpedoes.

Decals Common term for water-slide transfers found in almost all model kits.

Dihedral The angle of an aircraft's wing tip above the wing root. Opposite to anhedral.

Diorama Scenic backdrop for a model kit, or scale depiction of a specific scene. Can be small, consisting of just a few elements or very large, incorporating dozens or even hundreds of elements.

Drybrushing Modelling technique in which a brush with almost all the paint removed is applied to a model, in order to accentuate raised areas and mimic the effects of light reflecting off corners and edges.

Elevators Moving control surfaces on the tailplane of an aircraft.

Ejector pin mark Circular depression in the surface of a plastic part, caused by the metal pins that are used to remove the parts from the mould during the injection moulding process. A common kit fault that can be remedied through application of filler.

Filter A very thin wash applied over a large area or an entire model. Typically used either to tone down or bring out the base colour. Can also help to blend the different colours of a camouflage paint scheme.

Flaps Hinged control surfaces of an aircraft's wing or fuselage.

Flash A thin web or seam of plastic around the edge of a kit part, caused by ill-fitting or worn moulds. Can be easily removed with a modelling knife.

Floatplane Aircraft fitted with floats for waterborne take-offs and landings.

Flying wires Aircraft rigging between struts, spars and wing components of a monoplane, biplane or triplane.

Gauge Width between rails of a railway track or a size measurement of tools, wires, nuts, bolts etc.

Glacis Front, usually angled, plate of a tank.

Idler Non-driven wheel supporting one end of a tracked vehicle's (e.g. a tank's) tracks.

Injection moulding Common process used to produce virtually all commercial large-run plastic scale model kits. Molten plastic is injected into two or more close-fitting moulds and rapidly cooled before being ejected as a complete kit.

In-line engine Type of engine in which the cylinders are arranged in straight banks.

Island Main superstructure of an aircraft carrier.

Kitbashing Modelling slang term used to describe the process of combining parts of two or more kits to produce a single model.

Links The individual elements of a tank's tracks.

Mantlet (or mantle) Armoured gun housing of a tank, usually cast and part of the turret.

Muzzle-brake Fitting on the end of a gun barrel to regulate muzzle velocity, used to counter gun recoil and the tendency of a gun to rise during sustained or high-speed firing.

Nacelle Streamlined aircraft housing for an engine or radar array.

OOB Acronym; 'Out Of the Box'. Slang term used to describe a model completed from a single kit, without using any aftermarket parts or additional scratch-built modifications or upgrades.

Pannier Part of tank hull that overhangs the tracks, or additional stowage to a vehicle (e.g. a motorcycle).

Photo-etched parts Highly precise flat sheet of metal parts produced by a special photochemical process. Usually produced as aftermarket accessories, but also included in some high-end modern kits.

Pin wash Type of wash applied with a very small brush to specific areas of a model. Typically used to accentuate panel lines and other small details.

Plasticard Polystyrene sheet for modelling, available in various thicknesses. Very useful for scratch-building parts, making modifications, or carrying out kit conversions etc.

Port Left-hand side of a ship looking forward.

Prototype The first model of a production item, used to study, develop and present a future product. In modelling terms frequently used to refer to the full-size original of a particular model.

Pusher Aircraft arrangement in which the propeller is placed at the rear to drive the machine forward.

Radial engine Type of engine in which the cylinders are arranged around the drive shaft.

Resin A common term describing liquid plastics used for casting. Common types include urethanes, epoxy and polyester. Often used to produce small, specialist or short-run model kits or parts.

Return roller Small supporting wheels placed beneath the top run of a tank's tracks.

Rivet counter Slang name for a modeller who is particularly obsessive about ensuring absolute accuracy of detail.

Road wheel Main wheels of a tank or tracked vehicle, usually on sprung suspension.

Rotary engine Type of engine in which the cylinders actually revolved around the prop shaft.

Rotor The blades of a helicopter.

Roundel Term for circular markings that denote nationality of an aircraft.

Rudder Pivoted control surface at the rear of an aircraft or ship.

Runner Not often used, but the correct term for the thick plastic frame that holds the individual parts of an injection moulded model kit.

Scratch building Building either an entire model or a sub-assembly from 'scratch' rather than using kit parts. True scratch building involves manufacturing parts from basic materials; however it is also used to describe the process of altering kit parts so they can be used for a different purpose.

Silvering Undesirable 'frosted' sheen that appears on model decals applied to a matt painted surface, caused by tiny air bubbles trapped beneath the decal film, which is unable to conform to a matt finish. Solved by application of gloss varnish prior to decaling.

Sink mark Common kit fault in which a part features a depression in the surface of the plastic, caused by molten plastic not completely filling the mould during the injection moulding process. Can usually be remedied with filler, although if complex surface detail has been lost this can be difficult to reproduce.

Skirts Armour plates along the hull sides of a tank, usually employed to protect tracks and suspension.

Smoke projectors Stub-like fittings on the turret or superstructure of AFVs that fire smoke candles.

Solids Archaic term for the rough wooden model kits that were the predecessors of the modern plastic scale model kit.

Spaced armour False armoured surface placed in front of the superstructure of a tank to deflect or absorb shell fire etc.

Spar Round wooden, metal or composite pole used in the rigging of sailing ships to resist compressive and bending forces, and to provide support for the sails.

Spinner Cover for the centre boss of a propeller.

Sprocket Toothed drive wheel of a tank or tracked vehicle that engages the track to give propulsion. Usually placed at the front or rear of the chassis.

Sprue Strictly, the tabs of plastic that attach the plastic parts of a kit to the larger runners, but commonly used to refer to the complete plastic frame.

Squadron codes Numbers, letters or emblems used on military aircraft and vehicles to indicate the identity of a particular unit.

Starboard Right-hand side of a ship looking forward.

Stars and bars Colloquial term for insignia of the US military that features a horizontal bar either side of a five-pointed star.

Stem The forward part of a boat or ship; an extension of the keel itself that curves up to form the bows of the vessel.

Stern The rear or aft part of a boat or ship.

Stowage Generic term for equipment and kit lashed to the superstructure of a tank or military vehicle. Often added to models to provide interest and realism.

Stretched sprue Modelling technique used to produce fine plastic filaments for rigging, aerials etc., in which spare plastic sprue is heated over a flame and gently pulled apart.

Strut Structural component of an aircraft designed to resist longitudinal compression, often used in early aircraft to support wings and landing gear etc.

Super detailing The process of adding additional detail to a model beyond the parts included as standard in a kit. This may include detail that is missing or inaccurate, or replacing detail that is not of an adequate standard.

Thinner Solvent used to thin paint, improving consistency for modelling or for use in an airbrush, for example.

Transfer Archaic term for water-slide decals.

Transparency Generic term for clear plastic parts of a model kit – typically the cockpit canopy, gun turrets etc.

Tricycle undercarriage Type of aircraft landing gear configuration with a single wheel at the nose and two behind, rather than the more traditional tail-wheel type.

Turret Revolving gun housing on an AFV, aircraft or ship.

Turret ring Circular bearing on which a turret revolves.

Vacuforming Method of component production in which a plastic sheet is heated, stretched, and held against a pattern or mould by applying vacuum between the mould surface and the plastic sheet. Vacuforming is used to make hollow parts for models and frequently to make shaped transparent domes, canopies and windows.

Wash Term for a very thin coat of translucent paint. Normally used to highlight and shade details of a model.

Waterline model Model of a ship or submarine in which the hull is cut away to depict a vessel at sea. Often mounted on a baseboard or as part of a scenic diorama.

Weathering Term describing a range of techniques used to recreate a vehicle, aircraft or ship with a well-worn or used appearance. Typically this consists of adding dust, mud, rust, scratches, oil spills, smoke stains and similar realistic effects to a model.

White metal A metal alloy, often used to produce detailed figures, specialist kits and small aftermarket parts or accessories.

Yards Spars that cross the masts of a ship, used to support sails, rigging or radio or radar arrays.

INDEX